The Crash of the Dragonfly

Unbelievable Trials Lead to Unimaginable Blessings

Carolyn Searls

THE CRASH OF THE DRAGONFLY

Copyright © 2020 by Carolyn Searls

All Scripture quotations are taken from the Authorized King James Version.

ISBN: 978-1-952369-18-6

Cover design by: Katie Searls
Photographs provided by Rick Searls and Carolyn Searls
Book design by: EA Book Publishing

Published by EA Books Publishing, a division of Living Parables of Central Florida, Inc. a 501c3
EABooksPublishing.com

DEDICATION

My husband and I dedicate this book to L. Dale McCallister, our pastor who led us to a saving knowledge of Jesus Christ; ordained my husband into the ministry; supported our family, prayed for our ministry, and stood with us through thick and thin in the establishment of Brooke's Point Bible Church. He encouraged us to write this book about the mighty hand of God at work in building His church.

CONTENTS

FOREWORD

You should write a book. How many times do people say that when they talk to someone interesting, or hear of their experiences? Others and I have said those very words to Pastor Rick Searls as we listened to him share God's call upon his and his wife, Carolyn's lives. God directed them to serve Him as missionaries on the Island of Palawan in the Philippines. You hold in your hands that book we asked them to write.

I have known Pastor Searls and Carolyn nearly all of my life. I was a little boy when God called them to leave friends, family, and home to serve Him on a foreign field. I listened as Rick preached the Word in church and shared the call that God placed upon their lives. Today I still sit with that same boyish curiosity as they reveal ways God directed them and the events the Lord used in their lives.

Travel with the Searls family to Palawan and see firsthand the places they served, meet the Malacao family, and walk to the foothills of the mountains and see the trail Rick stumbled down to find medical attention. Visit the barrios and villages in the backwoods with them.

You have the same exciting privilege to share in those experiences as you read this book. Praise the Lord that when God called them, they responded to the words of the psalmist, "I made haste, and delayed not to keep thy commandments." (Psalm 119:60) They obeyed the Spirit's leading with purpose, seeking to please the Lord and bring Him the utmost glory. We truly serve a great God and this book is a testament to that truth.

Pastor Chris Brown
Maranatha Bible Church
Director, Maranatha Bible Missions.

ACKNOWLEDGMENTS

We praise the Lord for the man God used to lead my husband, Rick, and me to a saving knowledge of Jesus Christ, Pastor L. Dale McCallister, co-founder, pastor, and now Pastor Emeritus of Maranatha Bible Church (MBC) in Zanesville, OH. His passion for the Word of God was contagious. As young Christians he showed us the relevance of the Bible to everyday life. Questions we asked, he answered with the Scriptures. The support and guidance he gave to us cannot be measured.

Our hearts will forever be grateful for the love and encouragement we received from our home church family. Some not only prayed and gave, but visited us on the field and helped us in the work—Mrs. Edna Morrison, Ronald Smith, Paul Dawson, Donna Berger Mundy, Nancy Smith, and Kathie Collins Waddington. We appreciate all the churches and individuals who support the ministry in prayers and finances.

We can never repay the kindness shown to us by Rev. Gary and Edith Jones, our missionary friends, who welcomed us into their home each time Rick had to be in Manila for medical care due to chronic malaria.

To Scott, Brad, and Angie, our three children, we love you and thank you for your ministry to us and the people of Palawan as you served alongside us in the ministry. Your support meant everything to us.

The church would not be what it is without our faithful co-workers, Pastor Joe Malacao and his wife, Fe. We praise God for bringing us together as co-laborers in His harvest field along with their children who now carry on the work in leadership roles.

This book wouldn't be what it is without the help of my husband, Rick Searls. Most of the content in the book came from him and his personal experiences. He was a support to me throughout the years it took to write our missionary experiences. I'm grateful for my editorial team: Rhonda Robinson, my writing coach, and Suzette Jordan. A special recognition goes out to Ralph Koceja, Karen Silos, Kathy Godwin, and my Word Weavers Upstate group for the input they added to the book in its early stages.

- *Carolyn Searls*

INTRODUCTION

Rick and I lived across the world from Joe and Fe Malacao, yet God brought our lives together through unusual circumstances. We saw miraculous events take place as we served the Lord together in the southern part of the Island of Palawan, Philippines.

Over the past forty plus years, Rick and I have enjoyed the privilege to serve Christ through missionary aviation and church planting. Currently, Rick is the field representative for Southern Palawan Ministries (SPM) under Maranatha Bible Missions (MBM) out of MBC.

We trust you will see from the pages of this book how faithful and trustworthy God is. Whether it's through buffetings or blessings—successes or failures, He works through each one to bring good and receive glory for His namesake.

We experienced the truth that, "Ye are of God, little children, and have overcome them: because greater is He that is in you, than he that is in the world." (I John 4:4) The Lord is building His church, "and the gates of hell shall not prevail against it!" (Matthew 16:18)

It is our prayer that this book honors our great and marvelous God, and that it will be an encouragement to you to keep on keeping on in His strength. May God be praised!

- Pastor Rick and Carolyn Searls

CHAPTER ONE

When the Unexpected Happens

I awoke to bright blue skies and the smell of fresh, clean air after on-and-off rain showers of previous days. A glorious air of peace encompassed me on this faraway island. Winds were calm, barely moving the leaves on the banana trees that lined the flight base runway. I looked out the window of our thatched roof home and breathed in the beauty of this tropical paradise on the Philippine island of Palawan.

With clear blue skies above, it looked like a perfect morning for a flight. I watched my husband, Rick, walk to the open airplane hangar on base. Its cement floor and tin roof resembled a carport more than a hangar. He tied a rope to the front-wheel landing gear of the Super Cub he flew, and pulled the single-engine aircraft onto the manicured grass airstrip.

Rick told me today's mountain runway was considered a one-way strip because he could only land and take off in one direction. He had to maneuver the stick of the airplane to lift its nose up and keep the tail down at just the right angle to land uphill on the mountain's side. He had about thirty to forty feet in width and seven to eight hundred feet in length to set the plane down and taxi uphill to a flat section just above the village.

After a routine precheck of the plane's exterior and its engine, he called me on the shortwave radio inside our house, "618 departing fight base." The aircraft's number was 618.

I heard the roar of the engine and answered, "Roger, 618 departing flight base." Procedure required that I stay by the radio during all his flights so I'd know where to send help in case of an emergency—the last point of contact.

Once the plane took off from the plush green runway, I went back to the window of our nipa house and watched the plane ascend. Overlooking the banana trees stood impressive mountains that ran down the center of the banana-shaped island. Soon the small plane became a speck in the sky. I'd wait for Rick's next call, when he'd be on approach to land at the village.

Against all odds, Rick and I arrived on the field. Our three children, Scott age nine, Brad age five, and Angie fifteen months old would've had academic and social advantages at the Manila boarding school, but it was six hundred and fifty miles away and across a section of the South China Sea. We'd rarely see them.

Living in Manila would protect them from heavy exposure to malaria, but we felt the love, security, and emotional support we could provide as their parents in a foreign country also mattered.

We chose to homeschool our three children. This required a consistent dedication to them and their studies. A bonus of being home with us was they'd get to see tribal evangelism firsthand and share in it.

The purpose of today's flight was to bring a missionary's family to the flight base. His wife and two young boys would stay at the guest house while everyone else, including her husband and us, would be in Manila at an annual conference. We offered the place to her and she accepted without hesitation. Without the option of air support, she'd be in the mountain village alone with the tribe without medical care or a place to buy supplies. I felt her two young boys would relish the flat land of the base to play on instead of the hilly tribal village where they lived.

I had pancake batter in the refrigerator waiting to be fried when they returned. I wanted to treat the missionary's family and enjoy their company over breakfast.

Knowing Filipinos didn't feel satisfied without rice at every meal, I'd serve rice with the pancakes. It seemed strange to me, but I learned my lesson of not serving rice the hard way. I exchanged rice for macaroni and cheese one time. The young son of our guest eyed the food with a worried gaze. His sweet face looked up at his father and asked, "Daddy, where's the rice?" Embarrassed by his son's words, his father hushed him. But I was the one embarrassed.

I enjoyed preparing the guest house on base for their arrival. I swept the dust off the *swali* walls and split bamboo floors with a broom made of thin strips of bamboo tied together with twine. *Swali* walls were made from wide pieces of bamboo that had been softened and flattened then woven together. It helped that air could circulate through them since the heat could be suffocating.

I heard Rick's voice on the radio.

"618 on approach at Mt Saray."

"Roger, 618 on approach at Mt. Saray," I repeated in the handheld microphone.

Earlier Rick mentioned he checked the strength of the wind on flights to determine if it was safe to land by watching how the leaves blew and in what direction. I hoped the Palawano tribe had kept the grasses on the airstrip cut with their *bolos*. It had been a while since Rick had flown into that tribal station.

Two or three minutes after he reported he was on approach, the shortwave radio sounded again. "618 landed at Mt. Saray."

"Roger, 618 landed at Mt. Saray," feeling thankful he had a safe landing.

Safe landings weren't taken for granted. Each airstrip had been carved out of the mountainous forest. The tribes kept their village runway smooth to help prevent an accident.

Rick's military experience as a crew chief on an H-53 in Vietnam served him well as a jungle pilot. His role in missions was to support the missionaries living among the tribes in the jungles, and that's what he'd done for the Marines and soldiers on the ground in Vietnam. The small plane he flew on Palawan made living in the mountains a little easier for the missionaries and benefited the tribal people as well. He kept the plane ready at all times since he never knew when a medical emergency would come up.

One such medical flight involved a Palawano warrior who'd been accidentally struck in his right leg with a poisonous blow dart. It became infected to the point he could lose his leg. Rick flew him to the flight base, then drove him to the doctor in the town of Brooke's Point.

Some in the tribe felt the wounded tribesman should have asked the witch doctor to mediate between him and the evil spirits. They believed he was being punished for offending them. The witch doctor had the power to appease the anger of the spirits with the blood of the white chicken. But Rick flew the injured Palawano home with antibiotics that saved the man's leg and possibly his life.

Another medical flight involved a tribal lady who had a possible tumor in her abdomen. After transporting the woman and her companion to the doctor, Rick flew her back to her mountain home all smiles. Her supposed tumor turned out to be twin babies. The people teased her, "You must have eaten twin bananas." Two bananas sometimes grew together in the same rind. Palawanos have a saying that if you eat twin bananas, you will give birth to twins.

Another time I stared in dismay at a teenage daughter and her mother as Rick helped them out of the plane. The growth on the side of the girl's face looked the size of a baseball. Her clothes looked worn, ragged, and filthy. The doctor said she had an abscess and pulled all her teeth. Rick flew them back to their village with the necessary medication to heal.

I'd heard how excited the tribes in the mountains get at the arrival of the airplane, which they called Tutubi. Translated from Palawano into English it means dragonfly. When they heard the sound of the plane overhead, it sounded like a dragonfly to them. They also thought it looked like one because it had wings, a body, and landing gear that resembled legs with wheels—its feet.

Rick said a missionary told him when the Palawanos hear the plane they run to the airstrip shouting, "Tutubi is coming. Tutubi is coming." Rick could see them running to it from the air. I imagine that was his greeting on this morning's flight.

The Palawano Tribes

Poverty abounded among the tribes. They lived in some of the worst conditions Rick had ever seen. Their nipa huts were made of the same material as ours, except twine held the *swali* to the posts rather than nails. Their small huts stood off the ground on posts and the *swali* walls often looked crooked.

In our mission training, we were required to build a house in the forest with other missionary candidates from tree trunks and thick rolls of hefty green plastic like used for trash bags. We wrapped the plastic cover around the house's frame and tied it to the posts with baler twine. Our furniture had to be made with the same materials. God enabled us to accomplish something we had no idea how to do. That training made more sense now that we saw the homes of the mountain people.

The huts of the villagers are built on hills and close to a river where they can bathe, wash what little clothing they own, and gather water for cooking. Sometimes they had only a T-shirt and shorts and wore them until the cloth came apart. On one of Rick's visits with the villagers, he saw ladies pick lice out of each other's hair and pop the critters into their mouths, perhaps for the protein. For food, they grew root vegetables, rice, corn, and hunted for wild animals in the forest with homemade spears and blowguns. The blowgun and darts they'd given Rick as a gift stood in a corner of our home as a token of their gratitude for his service to them.

Rice remains their main source of livelihood. They trade it in the lowlands for clothing, blankets, and other supplies. As long as they have rice, they can survive, which means they count on a good harvest.

Tribal people lived as one unit and shared everything. It was necessary to survive. Privacy was not a consideration.

Rick had taken Scott and Brad on a previous flight to today's village. When he asked me how I felt about letting them go, I hesitated. I wanted to keep them safe at home with Angie and me. However, I also wanted them to experience the ministry of tribal evangelization. I reasoned that since the Lord had directed us into this ministry, I could trust Him to protect our children. I wanted them to enjoy serving alongside their dad.

When Rick surprised the boys and asked if they'd like to help him deliver supplies to the tribal village, the boys jumped with glee and shouted, "Yes," and took off running to the hangar. That surprise surpassed Christmas squeals of new toys. It thrilled me to see them so happy. Their school that day would be a field trip like none other.

Angie and I watched daddy take off with two extra happy faces aboard. When they returned from the mountains, we welcomed home two glad boys, one content father, plus a new family member, a red, green, and yellow parrot.

"I named him Jing," Scott said with eyes sparkling. He grabbed his bicycle and the little red wagon and managed to tie the handle of the wagon to his bike. With the parrot on his shoulder he pulled Brad around the base in the little wagon. I loved watching them be creative and enjoying life. Little Angie chased after them the best she could, laughing.

Another parrot was given to Brad. He named him Juicy Fruit. The boys had fun teaching them words like, "Hello, Goodbye," and "What's up?"

I felt good about letting the boys fly with their dad. Living life afraid of what could happen to our children was not an option for a productive and effective ministry. I didn't want to raise them to fear life but to embrace it and enjoy the adventures of missions, and life itself, in the opportunities God gave.

As our children grew, I wanted to give them freedom to get to know God and see what He can do for them, and not just hear what He's done for us. I prayed they'd see His goodness and experience His blessings personally.

It's not easy to let go. But what choice do we really have? So much of life is out of our control.

I asked Rick how the tribal people reacted to seeing white children. He said they glared at the boys with curiosity and were intrigued that they'd come. Any awkwardness the boys felt dissolved when the villagers handed them the colorful parrot. It showed their gratitude for the visit.

The reaction of the mountain people was similar to the reaction we had in town when we purchased supplies. If people weren't accustomed to seeing white people, they stared at us, pointed, and giggled. I felt like we were monkeys in a zoo where people lined up along the fence to watch. Not only did our white skin stand out, but our blonde hair and tall frames made me realize how foreign we looked to them. The realization that I was the foreigner in their land sunk in that instant.

A few small-framed, brown-skinned Palawanos with black hair and brown eyes were brave enough to come up and pinch our children's skin. Then they stepped back, huddled, and covered their mouths snickering. Even when our children frowned and cried out, "Ouch," they laughed, not taking their eyes off us.

They were curious about Angie and said, "The baby girl looks like a toy doll that walks. But why does she have white hair like an old person?"

Walking to the hardware store, the town reminded me of a scene out of an old Western movie. The cement block buildings were covered in dust. Searching for supplies to fill orders for the missionaries, challenged us. Supplies were limited, as were their doctors and medicines. One upgrade in town was that the main road had been paved years earlier. I didn't see cars in town, but *jeepneys*, trucks, and tricycles—a motorcycle with a sidecar— were everywhere. Most didn't have mufflers because the travel on the road had torn them off a long time ago.

Rick should call soon that he was ready for takeoff.

Before Rick would take off from a mountain village, his routine was to walk the airstrip to look for debris, potholes, or erosion from rains. Before starting the engine, he told me he opened the side window of the airplane and yelled, "Clear prop." The villagers knew what clear prop meant—stay away from the airplane and keep your children, dogs, and chickens back to avoid getting hurt.

Everything must have checked out today because the shortwave radio sounded with Rick's voice. "618 departing Mt. Saray."

"Roger, 618 departing Mt. Saray." I couldn't wait for them to arrive. I'd fry the pancake batter as soon as they landed at the base.

I looked forward to the companionship of the missionary's wife, another mother with young children. How was she coping living in a tribal village on this remote island? How did she spend her days? How did the tribe treat her and what were they like? Did she feel safe when the Palawano warriors warred against other tribes? I missed the circle of friends I had enjoyed in the United States and hoped she and I would develop a friendship.

It had been a while since I'd had someone to talk to that could relate to me. Our children would enjoy having playmates too. I imagined her boys and ours running around the flight base chasing the dog, Henry, climbing trees, building toy airplanes with scrap wood in the hangar, and playing with our two colorful parrots. I'd not worry about the snakes that occasionally showed up.

A Snake's Visit

One afternoon after lunch Rick looked out the side kitchen window and noticed Brad standing frozen in the cherry blossom tree. From the window Rick motioned for him to stay very still. I needed to remain calm too, because hanging on a branch below Brad was a venomous black cobra.

These types of cobras, although life threatening, were shy and would usually slither away and hide unless they felt threatened. In case you think I'm adventurous and brave, let me tell you I am not. I had to survive the wildlife of a remote island by faith in God's goodness and protection like anyone else would.

Outside the house, Rick grabbed a long stick and stood a couple yards from the tree. He tapped the ground a few times to divert the snake's attention from Brad. The space between Rick and the tree gave the snake room to escape. If it felt trapped it may have spewed its poisonous venom for self-protection.

Five-year-old Brad didn't utter a peep or move a muscle—good instinct. He kept staring at the snake below him. The tapping of the stick distracted the snake and it dropped from the tree and slithered away in haste to the tall grasses off the property. Rick helped Brad climb out of the tree and held him to the relief of us all. Did it stop him from climbing trees? Of course not.

Our family faced two choices while living on a distant island. We could trust the Lord or be tormented with constant fears of the unknown. Knowing the Lord had prepared us for this place gave me the confidence I needed to trust Him. You won't know the depth of courage and strength God can give you until you're put in circumstances that require it.

I awoke out of my daydreaming and realized Rick had not reported that he was airborne. He should have called back within a couple of minutes. Did he forget to notify me after takeoff? I waited for a brief moment, then tried to reach him.

"618, this is the flight base. Come in."

Silence.

Concern welled up in me. I knew he was rolling down the runway for takeoff on his previous call. Procedure required that he report to the base as soon as he was airborne. I waited, but no call came. I tried again.

"618, are you there?"

The deafening silence made me want to think the worst. I couldn't let my mind go there. The ten-minute flight had turned into thirty. Where was he?

Maybe the plane's radio isn't working, or he'd taken a different route home.

I decided to step away from the radio for a better view of the sky and went to the kitchen window where I could still hear the radio if he called.

My eyes searched the tranquil blue skies for his plane. It didn't seem right that the sky appeared so peaceful when my husband was missing. I strained my ears for the sound of the plane's engine, but a haunting stillness permeated the air. While my insides churned like butter, I forced myself to remain calm by God's grace for the sake of the children. If Rick called, he'd need me to be able to think straight in order to help him.

Is this really happening?

Scott joined me at the window, looked up in the bright blue skies and asked, "What's wrong, mommy?"

"I'm looking for your dad's plane, sweetheart. He should have landed back at the base by now."

Looking up at me with eyes full of both dread and hope he asked, "Did he crash? Mommy, is daddy dead?"

I paused, then whispered, "I don't know."

Something to Ponder

I once read that when faced with a crisis, your training, experience, and spiritual maturity influence how you react in the book "Suffering" by Paul David Tripp. If we can look back and reflect on God's faithfulness through a difficult time, it helps us when something else happens we aren't expecting. We can thank God for His preparation that enables us to endure it. What training, experience, and spiritual maturity can God use, or has He used to see you through your troubles? How has He comforted you?

When we've been able to show forth faith in the middle of a crisis and remain calm, it is because of His strength and grace at work in us. Our hearts soar with praise to our lovely Lord Jesus, who gives us hope through any calamity and fills us with His peace. "Be careful for nothing; but in everything by prayer and supplication with thanksgiving let your requests be made known unto God. And the peace of God, which passeth all understanding, shall keep your hearts and minds through Christ Jesus." (Philippians 4:6-7)

Prayer

Lord Jesus, keep my mind stayed on Thy truth. Help me face life in Your strength that I not be overtaken by unexpected circumstances. Because You know my future, I thank You for using trials to establish my faith that I can face challenges with courage. Truly You are a friend like no other. I surrender to Your plans for my life knowing that they are to give me an expected end with peace and not evil. I believe blessings can be born from trials when in Your hands. Thank You for showing me more of who You are and getting me through situations I don't like or want. Whatever the outcome, let me remember You are at work to bring all things together for good to those who love You. Bless me with a fresh vision of my God. I will rejoice in Your eternal faithfulness. May Your glory be my heart's utmost desire. For Jesus' name's sake I pray. Amen.

CHAPTER TWO

Coloring the Darkness

"618, this is the flight base. Come in please." I hoped Rick's voice would magically appear over the shortwave radio of the Super Cub. I'd waited forty-five minutes for a ten-minute flight. On our last point of contact, he reported he was rolling down the mountain airstrip on takeoff. He always called back within a couple minutes to let me know he was airborne—but not this time.

Scott stood with me at the open window in our *swali*-walled kitchen searching the skies for dad. His longing eyes looked into mine and said, "Mommy, if daddy is dead, he is with the Lord." He chose to say the one thing that could calm our troubled spirits.

An amazing amount of sustaining grace kept us from falling apart. The children needed me to stay composed—at least outwardly. My mind wanted to go down the path of what ifs, but I couldn't allow it. I tried to calm my inner trembling, took a deep breath, and waited.

After an hour passed with no news from Rick, reality sunk in and my aviation training for an emergency surfaced. I reached for the flight manual and reviewed what to do in the event of a plane crash.

Don't panic. *I had to maintain a sound mind in case Rick called and needed help.*

Stay by the radio. *If Rick needed to contact me, his only means to do so was by the shortwave radio.*

Don't leave the base. *If someone came to the base to give me news, or if he arrived, I had to be there.* Even if I could search for him, I had no idea how to get to the mountain village where he must have crashed on takeoff.

And lastly, pour yourself a cup of tea and wait. I sat in the *sala* with a cup of hot tea and watched Brad and Angie play quietly on our split bamboo floor close by my feet.

Having any direction in a crisis is helpful, even if it doesn't solve the problem. I felt so helpless and wished I could do something besides wait. Had Rick survived the plane crash? And what about the missionary's family who was aboard the plane? Stay calm I told myself.

A year before we arrived on the field, I had to deal with my fear of losing Rick. What I learned from that experience enabled me to guard my mind in this present unwanted circumstance and not lose hope. Christians aren't exempt from problems, but when they come, we are blessed with a Friend in Jesus, who draws close to us through it all.

I avoided going into shock and despair by remembering God's faithfulness through our preparation for the field. Memories began to flood in and occupied my mind.

It all began five and a half years earlier at the close of a missions conference, when our pastor said, "If the Spirit of God has spoken to anyone in the congregation about surrendering your life for missions, come forward."

My heart raced and I tried to make sense of the

hammering in my chest. *Is God calling me to be a missionary?* The idea seemed preposterous. Alarm bells went off in my head—*Warning, danger ahead!* I can't do mission work. Only seventeen months earlier, I'd trusted Christ as my personal Savior. Being a new Christian meant I had a lot more to learn about God and His ways before taking off to do mission work. Rick was also a new Christian.

I tried to persuade myself this was not the Spirit of God working in me, but my emotions. *Lord, missionaries are mature, stable Christians. It would take me ten years to be like that.*

Thump. Thump. Thump went the beat of my heart. The pounding intensified when I tried to calm myself by reasoning it away. I couldn't ignore it. I felt choked. If I didn't surrender to what the Spirit of God wanted, I'd drop over from lack of oxygen. But if I surrendered to God's call, my entire life would be turned upside down. Fear took hold of me and tried to squeeze my life into its tight grip. I couldn't let it govern my decision. When I surrendered my heart to the Lord and told Him I'd go into missions if it was what He wanted, the thumping stopped immediately.

I filled my lungs with a much-needed deep breath but was left with an unsettled feeling. I knew God wouldn't call me to the mission field without Rick. Going had to be his decision. I decided not to say anything about this until he approached me.

I hoped I had about six months to embrace the realization of God's call before Rick would tell me the Lord had spoken to him about missions. However, as soon as I settled the matter with the Lord, Rick turned and gave me a look that I understood all too well. Our eyes locked as he asked, "Will you go with me?"

My eyes widened, glued to his, too stunned to speak. The Spirit of God had already shown me what my answer had to be. I nodded in agreement. It seemed too soon in our Christian life to be surrendering to fulltime service, especially foreign missionary work, but that's what we did. Hand in hand we walked to the altar with the verse "Go ye into all the world, and preach the gospel to every creature," Mark 16:15, hanging behind the pulpit. Each forward step seemed to solidify God's call and the matter was forever settled in our hearts.

Going through the mental exercise of God's call assured me that whatever happened with the plane, it wasn't because we weren't following God's leading. In times like these, it's crucial to remember truth to quench the fiery darts of doubts.

I looked at the clock and saw that more than two hours had passed with no word from anyone. I mentally reviewed the sequence of events that led Rick into missionary aviation.

Experiencing God's Guidance

Rick had trained as a crew chief on an H-53 helicopter in the Marine Corps. The Lord protected him through four hundred and seventy-eight combat missions during his thirteen-months in Vietnam, and he still enjoyed the aviation field.

The following months after our call, we focused on discovering God's direction going forward. I felt insecure and full of questions. Rick said he could not assume God wanted him in aviation just because he enjoyed it. We sought counsel, but no one could tell us what God wanted for our lives. We sought answers through prayer and His Word.

Peace of mind about where we were to serve and what type of mission work we were to do came from Psalms 16:11: "Thou [God] wilt show me the path of life: in thy presence is fullness of joy: at thy right hand there are pleasures for evermore."

I didn't know how the Lord would show us the path of life. Nevertheless, believing that He would, relieved me of the pressure of trying to figure it out. This helped me face the future with more courage.

The verse also revealed to me that the source of my joy was in His presence, and with Him there are unending pleasures. Our home, family, friends, and church gave us so much joy that I didn't want to leave any of it. But understanding that God was the source of our joy meant joy would go with us wherever we went. My struggle to leave home wasn't completely removed, but this definitely helped.

I read the book **Shadow of the Almighty: The Life and Testament of Jim Elliot** written by his widow, Elizabeth. Jim was one of five missionaries killed by the people he'd gone to reach for Christ. The fact that missionaries died serving the Lord scared me. Would I lose Rick on the mission field? What about my children? Would they be safe?

Had it not been for the clear call of God, that book would have stopped me from missionary work. I feared disobeying God more than mission work and continued walking through the doors He opened with fear and trembling.

Perhaps you can identify. For now, a fear of Him kept me on the path of life He had planned for us, but one day I'd choose to serve Christ out of love for Him.

I needed to let go of the life I knew by making God's desires for my future my own. The Spirit of God brought a verse to memory, Galatians 2:20: "I am crucified with Christ: nevertheless I live; yet not I, but Christ liveth in me: and the life which I now live in the flesh I live by the faith of the Son of God, who loved me, and gave himself for me."

What I wanted wasn't the issue. Christ purchased me with His incorruptible blood when He died on the cross for my redemption. My life belonged to Him.

These following words from Jim Elliot emphasize an eternal view of life:

He is no fool who gives what he cannot keep to gain that which he cannot lose.

If we need to let go of a comfortable life now to serve Him, we are giving up what we can't take with us for something eternal we can't have taken from us. "Every one that hath forsaken houses, or brethren, or sisters, or father, or mother, or wife, or children, or lands, for my name's sake, shall receive an hundredfold, and shall inherit everlasting life." (Matthew 19:29)

Doing laundry one morning, a strong sense came over me to give our house to the Lord. I loved our home. However, I stopped what I was doing and knelt by the couch in submission.

On my knees I prayed, Lord, I *dedicate* our ...

The Spirit of God stopped me before I could get the word *house* out of my mouth, reminding me, He had not asked me to *dedicate* our house to Him but to *give* it to Him.

I started over. "Lord, I *give* You our home."

As I let go of things, it became easier for me to think about leaving home. Little by little my heart's desire was being changed to what the Lord Jesus wanted for my life.

The thought of failing the Lord troubled me, so I prayed for reassurance. *What if You send us into missions and we aren't able to complete the work You sent us to do? What if we quit when things get hard? If You Lord see we will begin this journey into missionary service but not be able to finish it, please do not take us one step further.*

Again, He answered me from Scripture. "Faithful is he that calleth you, who also will do it." In 1 Thessalonians 5:24 God promised His faithfulness would keep us faithful to His calling, and I took Him at His Word. Encouragement came when I decided that just as I had trusted Him in my salvation, I would trust Him in His call to missions. We sought further guidance from the Spirit of God through prayer and His Word.

Rick wrote to different aviation mission boards to know their requirements to become a missionary pilot. He read their brochures and saw he'd need an Airframe and Powerplant (A&P) license, a private pilot's license, and a commercial pilot's license. Most boards preferred their pilots be on the field by age thirty. Rick was twenty-six years old. He searched colleges offering specialized aviation training and found a school in Texas that offered a two-year program to acquire his A&P license. His pilot's licenses had to be acquired in his free time. This would work, but should we do it? We hesitated.

We had to know beyond a doubt that God wanted this because it meant quitting his job. How would we live? We had a baby and a four-year-old to support, plus a house payment until our house sold. As we sought the mind of the Lord, something extraordinary happened that allowed us to know the right decision.

I talked to the Lord one morning as I swept the carpet asking what we should do. *Father, do You want us to move for Rick to begin aviation school?* After I prayed a thought came to me.

If I (God) do not want Rick to go to school, I will close the door. Don't you shut the door.

Of course, the answer was so simple. If God didn't want Rick to train in aviation, He'd make it impossible for us to go. Believing this settled the matter for me. I could take the next step by His grace with assurance of His leading.

When Rick arrived home from work, he didn't make it to the top of our split foyer stairs, before I announced, "I've got something to tell you."

Without hesitation he replied, "I've got something to tell you first."

At the kitchen table I listened as he passionately

rehearsed, "You know how we've been praying about whether I should go to school. Well, I believe we should go because the Lord impressed upon me that *if God doesn't want me to go to school, He will close the door. I'm not to shut the door.*"

He looked at my face lit like a Christmas tree with a quizzical expression. "What is it you wanted to tell me?"

"What time of day did this happen?"

Perplexed as to why I'd ask such an irrelevant question, he answered, "I don't know the exact time, but sometime around 10:30 this morning because I was on break. Why?"

"I don't know the exact time either, but it was around 10:30 this morning while I swept the carpet that I had the exact same thought."

Recognition of what the Lord did crossed Rick's face. Assured of our next step, the house went on the market.

The Lord is patient with us as He takes us on a path that can be seen only through the eyes of faith. He welcomes our clasp to His unseen hand, while He holds our heart with His promises.

"And when he [God] putteth forth his own sheep, he goeth before them, and the sheep follow Him: for they know his voice." (John 10:4) We purposed in our hearts to follow Him, for we knew we had heard His voice.

With our two young sons, we pulled out of our driveway, even before our house sold, and headed to aviation school. As we drove away, I wanted to turn and take one last look at the home where I thought I would raise my children. The home where Rick had bowed his knees and accepted Christ as his Savior, and the place where we'd had lots of great times with family and our new Christian friends. Before I looked back, I remembered Lot's wife. I knew I wouldn't turn into a pillar of salt, but I couldn't go forward looking backwards.

Instead of beholding what was behind me, Rick, Scott, and I began to sing as we drove away with baby Brad in my arms, *I have decided to follow Jesus; no turning back, no turning back.*

The cord to life as we knew it had been cut.

When Trust Is All You Have

Three hours passed and I longed for word from Rick. Believing the Lord led him into missionary aviation made the plane crash puzzling.

When bad things happen, we can put ourselves on a guilt trip and think we're being punished for something. But Romans 8:1 says, "There is therefore now no condemnation to them which are in Christ Jesus, who walk not after the flesh, but after the Spirit." Whatever happens in your life, please know He loves you unconditionally. At times we need His purging that dross can be removed from our life to develop greater patience and increase our faith.

I knew God saw our current situation and heard our prayers because He is much more than a supernatural being somewhere far away in the sky. He's a personal God who loves us and was with us in our nipa hut. He was with Rick and the family in the plane, too. The Lord made this truth clear to me when Rick was studying aviation in Texas for the field.

Because our house hadn't sold before we moved for Rick's aviation training, it put us in a financial bind. Right or wrong, we thought he had to start school right away to be on the field by age thirty.

I awoke more than once in our two-bedroom Texas apartment to a bare refrigerator and empty cupboards. Usually I melted into tears, but not this time. Instead, I wrote out a grocery list and presented it to the Lord. I asked Him for a pound of hamburger, a dozen eggs, a loaf of bread, a gallon of milk, cereal, a few other items, plus bananas. I really like bananas, but I decided to scratch them off the list since we could do without them. They seemed like a luxury at a time like this.

I told no one about my list, not even Rick. I wanted him to be free to focus on his demanding studies. When he didn't have evening classes, he baked gingerbread and pecan pies for extra income. I babysat a couple children who attended the Bible club we held in our apartment. Several children made professions of faith and a few of their mothers.

Later that day, the father of the children I babysat knocked on my door. I greeted him and saw he held two brown bags of groceries in his arms. My friend's husband appeared nervous. He shuffled his feet and looked at the cement breezeway floor. "My wife told me you were going through a hard time. I received a bonus check at work today and wanted to help." His wife attended my discipleship class for new Christians. She must have noticed our shortage of food at the Bible study that morning.

Our neighbor came inside to set the groceries on our kitchen table. I tried my best not to cry. I didn't want to embarrass him. With a pasted smile on my face, tears fell down my cheeks, and he hurried out the door.

I unpacked the sacks to see cereal, hamburger, milk, eggs, bread, and the few other items on my list—only doubled! Everything on my list sat before me including one bunch of bananas. I stared at them with happy tears and saw God's tender heart towards me. I noted that the bunch of bananas weren't doubled and knew why. I'd removed them from the list. Nothing was purchased by our friend *except* the items on my list. The man hadn't seen the list or even known I had one. No one knew—no one except the Lord.

The bunch of bananas spoke of God's goodness and unconditional love. He knows all and hears our prayers. My love for Him grew with each glorious bite of banana. "Casting all your care upon him; for he careth for you." First Peter 5:7 came alive. I didn't need bananas, but He wanted me to see what kind of God He is. Rick was studying to serve Him, but He served us through a friend.

Feeling overjoyed at God's provision, I shared the exciting news with our local pastor. He wondered why I'd asked for hamburger when God owns the cattle on a thousand hills. Had I limited God? How well did I really know Him?

The next time we ran out of food, I didn't pray for food. Because God had been so good to us, I prayed, *Father, we've never missed a meal. If this one time you want us to go without, it's okay.* Then I set the table. Granted there was no food to serve, but what if God chose to feed us? I'd be prepared.

Rick would be home from classes in about five minutes for supper. I had no food to feed him, or the children, but I was fine. We'd survive. Just then I heard a knock at the door. A southern gentleman whom Rick had talked to about Christ stood in front of me holding a large pot and a cloth-covered pan. Beaming with pride, he stretched out his arms of food and said, "I made my special recipe of black-eyed peas and Louisiana cornbread and want you to taste it."

He had no idea he was sent there by the Lord or that we had no food.

"We'd be happy to taste your black-eyed peas and cornbread," I said as I motioned him towards the already set table. I don't know who smiled more, him or me. After he left, I shared a chuckle with the Lord, *You not only provided the food but had someone cook it for me too. Thank You, Lord.* He does so much more than we can imagine.

A couple minutes after he left Rick walked in the door with no idea what had just transpired. I didn't want to tell him yet but first behold my family enjoying the food. Gratitude flooded my soul watching them, but I had to laugh when Rick said, "These are the best beans I've ever eaten." He didn't like beans.

I remembered what my local pastor said about God owning the cattle on a thousand hills and decided to start praying for steak, not because I wanted to eat it as much as I wanted to show the Lord, I could trust Him for more than hamburger. Soon our freezer filled with steaks given by friends. For the next two years we ate all the free steak we wanted. We celebrated this provision by inviting the pastor and his wife to a steak dinner. We didn't need steak, but our faith needed to be increased in our God.

Through adversity my relationship with Christ grew as I experienced "My Beloved is mine, and I am His." (Song of Solomon 2:16) Although funds remained scarce, I felt rich in the things the Lord taught me and the souls He'd given us.

Remembering God's miraculous and personal care through His past provisions sustained me in the present.

Although four hours had passed since I'd last heard from Rick, it felt like time had stopped. I held onto hope that he was still alive. But if not, the Word of God says to those who are His, "to be absent from the body is to be present with the Lord." (2 Corinthians 5:8) Was he seriously injured, or with the Lord? I couldn't call anyone. There weren't telephones, email, or iPhones, so I went back to the radio.

"618, are you there? Come in please." Silence. My heart was in my throat. What did the future hold? Was there a future with Rick? He'd been in my life since the eighth grade.

I colored the darkness with what I knew to be true. No matter what the outcome, all would be well. Knowing how faithful the Spirit of God had been to lead and care for us in the past calmed my troubled spirit in the present. By focusing my mind on truth, hope arose out of the darkness.

Something to Ponder

There are times the Lord impresses upon us to do something we feel is not possible and completely out of our comfort zone. The process the Spirit of God takes us through can be difficult, scary, and filled with uncertainty. Do we allow Him to grow our faith, or decline the invitation to live by faith? It's rewarding if we can let Him reveal Himself to us in ways we hadn't known Him. It's not easy to face a future out of our control, or to go without food to feed our family, or be in situations that seem unsafe for our children. But if the Lord is guiding us on this path, He will take care of us and expand our personal relationship with Him until all we can see is how awesome He is. He does the impossible—just for us, His children. Miracle after miracle happens under His care, for nothing in our lives escapes His knowledge. He understands our needs, even our wants, and enjoys meeting them, like we do for our own children. "Oh, taste and see that the Lord is good." (Psalm 34:8) Have you found the joy-filled life He gives far surpasses the temporary happiness found in time-based things of this life?

Prayer

Heavenly Father, I love You. I want to follow You and appreciate Your leading in my life. You are good and true to Your promises. May Your will be my utmost desire. Grant me courage to walk with You through the dark days knowing You are trustworthy. Help me not fear the future but understand You are there and will be with me in the unknowns. Replace my doubts with faith, my insecurities with confidence, and teach me more of You that my understanding of Your greatness and glory can be revealed through my life. I ask these things in Jesus' name. Amen.

CHAPTER THREE

Facing Our Fears

My deepest fear was losing Rick on the mission field. I couldn't imagine life without him. As I waited to find out if he'd survived the plane crash, I felt grateful that the Lord prepared me ahead of time to face the possible death of my husband.

A Threatened Future

Two years earlier Rick spent eight months in jungle pilot training doing mechanical work on airplanes and short-field landings in and out of dead-end canyons. Only one more month of training and he'd be assigned to an overseas mission field. We looked forward to finding out where we'd be going, like a child looks forward to birthdays. This is the moment we'd been working towards since we left our Ohio home almost four years earlier. It appeared we'd reach our goal of being on the field when Rick turned thirty years old in May.

Our blonde-haired, blue-eyed baby girl was born close to the same time as Rick would graduate, May of 1978. She stole our hearts. At the hospital Rick bent over to kiss her but had to grab his stomach and hold it with tight fists. A stabbing pain shot through him and his face turned pale. We hoped a good night's rest would cure whatever it was.

When home, he noticed his bowels turned a bright yellow color, which freaked us out. We didn't know what it meant. He clutched his stomach often and grew weaker every day. With less than four weeks of training left, my strong Marine lay in bed, unable to work. I'd never seen him like this.

After three weeks of being in bed, instead of Rick being assigned to a mission field, he had to step out of the flight program to seek medical help and give his body time to heal. Our home church flew us to Ohio, where we'd have the support of family and friends. The pastor arranged for us to stay in a beautiful A-framed house nestled in a picturesque setting in a wooded countryside. In this quiet retreat he had the perfect place to rest and heal. Nonetheless, I felt alone and confused and couldn't enjoy the beautiful scenery and rustic home.

Seeing Rick in bed with no improvement drained my energy and hope for his recovery. I became anxious and uncertain. I always admired his strength and felt safe with him. Now I needed God's strength so I could be strong for him and care for the children while he slept through each day, which turned into weeks and then months.

My heart grieved as I watched my husband's health deteriorate. His body could not absorb nutrients from the foods he ate. Weakness kept him from being able to hold our baby daughter for fear of dropping her.

I took him to see doctors, but no diagnosis could be determined. I dreaded the thought of losing Rick and my faith hit a crossroad. Could I trust the Lord when I couldn't see a reason for what was happening? I lived in a dark place where God seemed silent. This unfamiliar and difficult journey challenged my faith. I didn't know a good God would allow such suffering when you've been obedient to His leading.

Had I done something to anger God? What puzzled me most was why the Lord led Rick to aviation school in Texas and the mission board's training programs if He wasn't going to use any of it for ministry. From a place of uncertainty, I reminded the Lord that going into missionary work had not been our idea.

The challenges we'd experienced up to this point I'd accepted because I saw them as part of our training for missionary service in a foreign country. But this illness made no sense to me.

In the Book of Job, I read about a godly man who suffered the loss of his children, his servants, his home, his wealth, and his health. He wished he'd never been born. But we see Job trusted the Lord through it when he said, "Shall we receive good at the hand of God, and shall we not receive evil?" (Job 2:10) He knew God saw his heart and life and concluded, "When he [God] hath tried me, I shall come forth as gold." (Job 23:10)

Job's faith was gravely tested, but God is good and gave all Job lost back to him, only doubled. Job 42:10 says, "And the Lord gave Job twice as much as he had before." Job and his wife bore more children and those he'd lost were very much alive in heaven. He's with them today and will be eternally. What a hope we have as God's children by faith.

My faith was being tested through Rick's illness. I knew God loved me and was good, but it didn't feel like it. After all, He was the God who tenderly provided bananas for me. But I was about to learn He is also a supreme God, who rules. He is perfect in all His ways and He isn't only my Friend, He is Lord.

Three months passed and it looked like Rick might die. I cried out to the God of heaven, "Father, comfort me through Thy Word. Help me see You and find hope." The Spirit of God ministered to me through the following passages.

"Thus saith God the Lord, he that created the heavens, . . . I the Lord have called thee in righteousness, and will hold thine hand, and will keep thee, and give thee . . . for a light of the Gentiles; To open the blind eyes, to bring out the prisoners from the prison, and them that sit in darkness out of the prison house. I am the Lord. Behold, the former things are come to pass, and new things do I declare: before they spring forth I tell you of them." (Isaiah 42:5-9)

I understood the passage spoke of the coming Messiah, but the Spirit of God used these verses to show me He had not changed His plans for us regarding missionary service. However, I looked at Rick's emaciated body and asked, "How can this be? Was I making Scripture say what I wanted to believe, or had this really been God's Spirit encouraging me?"

In unbelief, I chose to believe Rick being well enough to ever go to the mission field was my wishful thinking, not God's Spirit speaking to me. I didn't realize at the time what a bad mistake I'd made. Without faith in God's Word, hope is lost and turmoil with heightened fear worms its way in and removes God's peace of mind.

Kneeling beside Rick's bedside, I begged God with tears and pleaded many times for his healing. My desire to see my husband well surpassed what God wanted. I was too scared to pray the words, "Nevertheless not my will, but thine, be done." (Luke 22:42)

After four months of chronic suffering with no change, Rick decided to get out of bed and make an effort to rejoin life. He'd figure out how to function

31

in spite of the sharp, stabbing pains. He walked to gain strength and found he could go one block before he had to quit.

He often went to church as he found it to be a refuge for his soul and eased the pain as the Word was preached and testimonies of God's faithfulness from the congregation were shared. I remember sitting in church crying; when people started telling what God had done for them, and my tears dried.

One Sunday evening when Rick was unable to attend church, I listened to our pastor, Dale McCallister, tell the congregation, "Rick is going to take the gospel to people who've never heard of the Lord Jesus Christ. Of course, Satan would attack him. Think people!"

I carried these words with me because they spoke of a hope for a future with Rick serving Christ.

After seven months of malabsorption, blood loss, and chronic pain, Rick looked sunken and thin with dark circles around his eyes. He ended up at the Cleveland Clinic. His older roommate told him to serve the Lord while he is young. The man's words gave me another glimpse of hope that maybe the Lord still wanted to use our lives in missions. These are little nuggets God sends our way to lift us over the rough rocks and hills that we have no strength to climb.

After numerous tests at the clinic in Cleveland, the doctors focused on Rick's pancreas. It produced only five percent of the enzymes the body needed to digest foods. There was no medical reason for this health issue, nor was there a cure. The doctors told him to eat a special diet of no fats and take enzyme supplements the rest of his life.

Would he be weak and in pain the rest of his life? I wasn't prepared for a life of watching him suffer. I wanted to go to sleep and let my mother take care of the children. Someone could wake me up to let me know how it turned out.

Instead of allowing my feelings of despair to take over, I dug into God's Word and studied it daily for spiritual strength. I couldn't stay focused by just reading it. If I gave into my feelings, it would be like calling God a liar because His Word says His grace is sufficient for me. We had to live by faith in our heavenly Father for hope to remain alive.

Rick and I didn't know how we could still possess an inescapable sense that God still planned to send us to the foreign mission field, but we did. He never complained throughout all his suffering but quietly accepted his condition. I asked him how he stayed strong in spirit.

He replied, "Early on I realized I could not allow my mind to depart from God's promises that He'd placed in my heart. When doubts and fears set in, I focused on His promises. Praying with you and holding onto one another with His promises close to our hearts gave me hope that one day this pain would leave me. I never doubted God's call into missions and will wait on Him to bring about the future He has for us."

How blessed I was to be married to a man like him. I depended upon him more than I realized. How could I live without him? He grounded me.

We were constantly in an attitude of prayer, seeking the Lord for strength and guidance. We read, "Trust in the Lord with all thine heart; and lean not unto thine own understanding. In all thy ways acknowledge him, and he shall direct thy paths." (Proverbs 3:5-6) That promise gave clarity in the midst of our perplexing circumstances. The verse directed us to wait on Him to show us the way forward, and that's what we did.

A few weeks passed since the nature of Rick's illness was known when a friend at church said, "God laid it on my heart to give you this money so you can return to complete your missionary flight training."

When Rick showed me the money for the trip back, my reaction was identical to his. *What? How is that possible?* For a moment we stood silent, staring at the money in Rick's hand. He wasn't able to do the work if we returned now, but maybe the Lord wanted us to trust Him and return in faith because He planned to heal Rick. But there was no way we could know that.

Rick believed the Lord was directing us to move back to jungle flight training and finish the course. I agreed, but there was no logic in it. He called the flight instructor and informed him we'd be returning in January of 1979, nine months after we'd stepped out of the program.

The Trip Back That Almost Wasn't

On our drive back to training, the freeway traffic was heavy and snow had begun to fall. All seemed well as the children watched the snow until a semi driver alarmed us by blowing his horn loud and long at us. We looked up to a frantic man waving his arm for us to get off the freeway.

Once on the berm Rick examined the vehicle and saw the axle on the U-Haul was about to break. We had no idea of the danger we were in and thanked God for the semi driver's warning.

Rick inched off the exit towards the dealership. As soon as we pulled into its entryway the axle broke and the wheel fell off. That was a close call. A team of workers transferred our belongings to another U-Haul and we were back on the road in an hour. Rick wanted to reach a certain town before stopping for the day, and the Marine in him never stopped short of his goal.

The farther we traveled, the thicker the snowfall became until we couldn't see the road ahead. We were in a blizzard. But where we were headed was only another hour's drive. Would Rick keep going? I prayed not. I felt a big relief when he pulled off the nearest exit for the night and located the only motel in sight. Had he tried to drive another hour to reach his goal, we'd been at the exact spot at the exact time the blizzard took the lives of six people. So many cars became stranded that the interstate had to be shut down for two days.

We thanked God that we were safe and warm in the motel. What seemed like a setback when the axle broke may have saved our lives. Our precious young children were cuddled in warm beds and not stranded in a cold car.

During those two days in the motel, raw cramps in Rick's abdomen made him wonder if he'd made the right decision to return to training. We knew this was a problem before we left, but we started this journey by faith hoping the Lord planned to heal him.

When we don't know the right decision to make, our pastor taught us to ask ourselves, *what brings God the most glory?*

Since neither of us wanted to give up, Rick felt it would be more of an encouragement to our church family and honor the Lord more to finish our trip to complete the training and see what the Lord did after we were there. We'd never know what might be if we turned around now.

To stay strong in faith, I thought of truth. *God remains faithful, and this too shall pass. Nothing in this life is eternal.* When facing doubts, preach truth to yourself.

Back at the flight base Rick did the best he could to complete his daily assignments. He went straight to bed when he got home. His health hadn't gotten any better. I lay on the bed beside him and uttered words that had been long in my heart, but I was too afraid to speak. "I don't want you to die."

With gentleness he responded, "But if I died, I'd be free of this pain. I'm ready to go home to heaven. God has given me a good life."

I cried.

It was time for me to let go and accept what I couldn't change. Selfishly, I didn't want to let him go and sought comfort from the Scriptures.

"Fear not; . . . neither be thou confounded; for thou . . . shalt not remember the reproach of thy *widowhood* any more. For *thy Maker is thine husband*; the Lord of hosts is his name; and thy Redeemer the Holy One of Israel; The God of the whole earth shall he be called. For the Lord hath called thee as a woman forsaken and grieved in spirit, and a wife of youth, when thou wast refused, saith thy God. For a small moment have I forsaken thee; but with great mercies will I gather thee." (Isaiah 54:4-7, *italics mine*)

These verses assured me that His grace would be sufficient if He took Rick to heaven. In them was the promise of protection over the children and me. By the grace God gives I could learn to live dependent upon the Lord without Rick, as hard as that would be, as He would be a husband to me. From His love I'd receive His protection, provision, and guidance.

Christ was not all I wanted, but He was all I needed.

My heart soared with grace and peace from the Spirit of God. The chronic condition of Rick's had been like a weapon used against us. But as Isaiah 54:17 says, "No weapon that is formed against thee shall prosper." This illness would not have its way with our lives because of our great and merciful God, even if God chose to deliver Rick through death.

Rick's lingering illness caused us to reevaluate what the Lord wanted. He hadn't healed Rick's body and he was too weak to suitably do the work. If we stepped away from missions, our consolation would come from knowing we'd never have to question if we'd trusted the Lord and returned to the training what would've happened, because we'd done that. Our determination to be obedient to Him had brought us to this crossroads.

Rick and I sat together in the living room of our small duplex and faced the facts; the Lord had not restored his strength or healed his body. Although we didn't want to abandon God's call, we had no choice. His physical stamina wouldn't hold up to the demands of a jungle pilot. We agreed he would resign from the training and we'd go home to Ohio permanently.

But as soon as we made that decision, eight-year-old Scott hurried out of his bedroom holding his big black Bible opened to a verse. His eyes bright with discovery declared, "Mom, Dad, listen. 'Ye are of God, little children, and have overcome them: because greater is he that is in you, than he that is in the world.' (1 John 4:4) Isn't that a great verse." He waited, excited for our reply.

With only a glance at each other, Rick and I knew the Lord didn't want us to quit. The best way I can explain how we knew this is by sharing the same verse in John 10:27: "My sheep hear my voice, and I know them, and they follow me."

From that time on we believed God was going to do something special in regards to enabling Rick to accomplish His task. The next day he went back to work at the flight base, although there was no change in his health. The instructors in the flight program had taken notice of Rick's condition and were contemplating what to do.

In the meantime, a couple in the same training program told us about a book on nutrition. I studied the book to see what it said could help the pancreas. Inside was a strange recipe full of nutrients to drink to feed the pancreas. When you're desperate, you'll try anything. Rick was a cooperative patient and drank the horrible tasting concoction I made for him daily.

To our delight, strength began to return to his body. In one week, all his pain subsided after ten months of suffering. He continued drinking the mixture and six weeks later all his complications with malabsorption and loss of blood healed. God used this substance to nourish and restore his health. We believe God healed him and used the drink to do it. Otherwise, the shake would've been in vain.

I'm always amazed at God's timing. The flight instructors met with Rick in the middle of the six-week healing period to talk to him about his health. When he told them that he believed the Lord was healing his body, they were glad. They had planned to ask him to step out of the program. But since his body was healing, they wanted him to stay.

A couple months later a medical doctor examined Rick. The doctor looked a little surprised when he informed him, "Your pancreas appears to be healing itself." Instead of quitting missions, Rick quit taking enzymes and eating a fat-free diet. God amazes me.

Beware of Traps

At our lowest point, when we felt we couldn't continue with the flight training or missions, some suggested it wasn't the Lord who led us, but we just wanted to be big shot missionaries. My view of a missionary was anything but a big shot. Perhaps some of the misunderstandings came from us not sharing the details of Rick's illness.

A few claimed we were never called, and another sent us an anonymous article indicating Rick behaved like a hypochondriac. We were told the Apostle Paul never despaired of life like we had. An acquaintance questioned if Rick had what it took to be a missionary, while others were concerned that we didn't know what we were doing. We didn't. But God did. How can a man know his way when the Lord directs his steps? We needed their prayers, not their judgments. It's so typical of human nature to try to make sense of something that makes no sense. They know God isn't the problem, so it had to be the person.

I remembered Job's extreme trial ended when he prayed for his friends. I knew when I read Job 42:10 that I did not want to extend my trial because of unforgiveness. I chose to hold no grudges. I couldn't understand what was happening through the things we suffered, so how could I expect others to.

What can we learn from criticism? To be careful judging God's leading in another man's life, for one. Life is messy and we all must depend upon the Lord to guide us through its maze as we pray for one another.

If you know God has called you, continue to move forward in the Spirit's strength as God leads. Don't give in to the devil's tactics to sidetrack you with unforgiveness or make you feel defeated. Rather, use negative comments to learn how to forgive, and reevaluate your life. There's no need for us to defend ourselves to one another because the Lord is our defense. He will show what's true in His time. Some will speak well of us and our ministry, and others will not. Pay it no mind, but keep our eyes on the Lord and press on.

Something to Ponder

Facing our fears allows us the joy of overcoming them by entering into the fear. Only God could have taken me through a period of time where I lived life as I would as a widow for a few months. It's not the same as death, but I faced the possibility of it and learned to find Christ is enough. The Lord showed me that Rick's healing came not because of all my begging, pleading, or crying, but because He is God; He is Sovereign; and it was His will. Through this affliction I learned to let God be God and submit to His supreme authority, whatever the outcome.

Facing the unknown can be frightening, but it helps to know that God works from an eternal perspective out of a heart of pure love for us. "Wherefore seeing we also are compassed about with so great a cloud of witnesses, let us lay aside every weight, and the sin which doth so easily beset us, and let us run with patience the race that is set before us." (Hebrews 12:1-2)

Prayer

Heavenly Father, thank You for Your faithfulness that's new every morning. Even during times when my faith seems small Your love, mercy, and grace sustain me. In Jesus' name I ask for the ability to trust You in all situations, good or bad. When suffering, let me remember You can turn it for my good and use it for Your glory. Through trials my faith is strengthened and my knowledge of You deepens. Grant me a heart to accept life the way You have planned it for me. Thank You for taking me through experiences to better equip me for Your service. Keep at the forefront of my mind the truth that You work from an eternal perspective to prepare me for heaven. I am thankful for Your constant presence and grace. Amen.

CHAPTER FOUR

The Impossible Made Possible

Five hours passed since Rick reported he was on takeoff from the tribal village in the mountains, which should have been a ten-minute flight. I'd stayed close by the short-wave radio in case he called. The children huddled near me while we waited for news.

I decided to try to call the plane's radio—again. The former missionary pilot on Palawan heard me from his airplane on another island. He answered his radio to advise me to switch channels and call the missionary's shortwave radio in the village. It was worth a try.

I changed channels but didn't expect anyone to answer because the radio sat inside the missionary's hut, and he was in Manila and his family in the plane crash. *Maybe a tribal member would hear me calling and know to push the button down on the receiver to answer it.*

I held the mouthpiece in my hand and called the missionary's radio. "This is the flight base. Come in, please." My insides fluttered like butterflies as I let go of the button to listen for a response.

Sparks shot through me like fireworks when I heard the voice of the missionary's wife on the other end. My heart cried out *she's alive!* feeling stunned and relieved to hear her voice. She said, "Carolyn, we crashed on take-off. The boys and I survived the crash with only a bump on the head of one of the boys."

I braced myself to hear what she'd tell me about Rick.

With the sound of urgency in her tone she began, "Carolyn, please pray for Rick. He's losing a lot of blood. The only way down the mountain is by foot. Palawano warriors are guiding him to the lowlands." She repeated, "Pray for Rick. He's losing a lot of blood," before we signed off the radio.

I paused for a moment to try to comprehend everything she said. Rick was alive and they were okay. *Thank you, Lord.* As she spoke, I tried to hold onto every word. Still, I found it hard to absorb all she said because my mind kept going to Rick's alive. Then to, "He's losing a lot of blood. Pray for him."

How badly injured was he? The good news—he was able to hike out of the mountain. He can walk. I prayed for the Lord to watch over him as he made his way home. The children heard the happy news and were grateful to know daddy was on his way home, but I remained guarded since I didn't know what to expect when he got back.

If I knew where to find the path down the mountain and the lowland village it led to, I'd have gone there in the jeep to help him. Four and a half hours after being told he was on his way home, and nine and a half hours since he'd left that morning, I looked out front to see a *jeepney* racing towards our front steps. Rick hobbled out, and the *jeepney* driver drove off in a hurry.

Rick limped up the wooden slats onto the split bamboo porch and into the *sala* holding a bloody cloth to his face. I stared at his dirt-spattered face, dilated pupils, bent stature, and torn clothing. His short, quick breaths told me he was in shock. Large holes in his light blue, stained jeans revealed his burned knees.

The children and I wanted to rush to embrace him, but immediately realized we had to stand back. He needed us to approach him with gentleness. He'd been in a fight for his life. It may have caused flashbacks from the time he fought in Vietnam.

The moment he stepped inside the *sala*, we heard the former pilot call on the shortwave radio. Rick said he wanted to take the call.

Still holding the bloody cloth to his worn face, he stepped on the first step down into the radio room and his ankle buckled. He'd sprained it in the crash and fell to the floor as his back hit the wooden steps. Managing to get off the floor, he answered the call. The pilot told Rick he needed to get the airplane out of the jungle, especially the engine. Rick agreed and understood its importance, but he needed to get to Dr. Laceste's for now.

Rick staggered feebly inside the doctor's office, holding onto me with each step. The doctor greeted Rick with a bewildered grin and asked, "What did you do to yourself?"

"I had a plane crash," he weakly replied.

Upon examination, Dr. Laceste said Rick needed surgery and ordered him upstairs to the operating room.

Rick faltered. "I don't think I can climb the stairs."

As if the doctor's abruptness could enable Rick to climb the steep open stairs, he snapped, "Get upstairs."

There was no other way for Rick to get to the operating room. He had to manage the stairs. Together we began the ascent with Rick's arm still over my shoulder for support. He sluggishly put one foot on a step and pulled the other one up beside it until we stood in the open operating room. Rick lay down on the sheet of plywood held up by four wood posts at the front of the room. We waited for the doctor, a trained anesthesiologist who had to become a surgeon in times like these.

It was six o'clock and like every night of the year, it got dark at 6:00 p.m. There was no electricity because of a broken generator. Brownouts happened so often that Dr. Laceste, who Rick affectionately called Doc Joe, taught himself to do surgeries with a flashlight in his mouth.

The flashlight batteries were low, so the doctor banged it a few times with his hand until a faint light appeared. The light kept fading so he did this over and over again while he sewed the gash on Rick's face below his nose shut. The Lord had to have stopped or slowed the bleeding before Rick got to the doctor or he would have bled to death.

With surgery complete, we went home and comforted the children as we tucked them inside their mosquito-net-covered beds with a prayer of thanksgiving. Exhaustion set in and this time Rick crashed onto his foam-pad bed. It felt welcoming and restful. I wanted to know the details of the plane crash, but now was not the time to ask.

It felt strange to wake up the next morning and know everything had changed. There would be no flights. Rick requested the missionary's wife and children be checked by Dr. Laceste and also asked for the Philippine marines to assist them out of the mountains. She didn't want to hike out with him the previous day. The marines helped them down the mountain to the doctor, where they all checked out good. We helped them settle in at the guest house on the base, then left for Manila to attend the annual conference.

Warriors, a Motorcycle, and a Jeepney

When back on the island, Rick drove me to the lowlands where the Palawano warriors guided him after the crash. Standing there, he pointed to a distant area in the mountains to show me where the plane went down. He was ready to tell me the whole story of the plane crash and began sharing the details.

"As usual I walked the runway before taking off. It rained on and off the past few days, so I looked for any erosion or debris on the grass airstrip. Not seeing a problem, I boarded my passengers and did the routine precheck of the engine. Everything checked out, so I reported to the flight base that I was departing the mountain airstrip. On takeoff, to my horror, I felt the front wheel hit a rut in the ground. The front of the airplane dipped forward and damaged the propeller. I lost crucial airspeed and only had seconds to decide what to do. I wanted to stop the plane, but it was going too fast and the runway was too short. I looked to my left and saw large boulders. On my right the Palawanos were lined up to watch the plane take off. The only option left was to fly off the mountain's cliff with a bent propeller and pray. I hoped the wind would get underneath the wings and allow the plane to glide to a safe landing on the beach, but what happened next should have killed us.

"Gliding to the beach was short-lived because once the plane flew off the cliff a large tree stood directly in front of us. Without airspeed, I could not get above or around it. Hitting it head-on was unavoidable. I braced for the direct hit, believing I would wake up in glory. But to lessen the impact, I pulled the nose up as much as I could before we hit. As the plane went through the tree's branches, everything seemed to happen in slow motion. A serene quietness came over me and I didn't feel the

45

impact of the hit at first. I sensed the peace of God, and expected to enter into the presence of the Lord any second. But in the next moment, I began to hear the propeller cutting through the branches of the top of the tree. Some went through the plexiglass windshield and shattered it."

"Is that how your face got cut?"

"Probably. Pieces of the windshield came at my face. At the same time, I heard the fabric of the plane's wings and fuselage tear. Then I felt the aircraft hit the side of the mountain with a hard boom. It slid partway down the mountain and stopped. We had no time to waste and needed to get out of the airplane as soon as possible. I turned to open the door, but it was jammed. The wing bolts had sheared and caused the wing to drop down and block the only door out of the plane. We were trapped.

"I looked for another way out and saw the shattered windshield left an opening that I could crawl out. I managed to escape out the window onto the hot engine. It burned holes into my jeans and scorched my knees, but I barely noticed until later because the main concern was the family. I had to get them out of the plane quickly because I saw fuel leaking onto the engine.

"As soon as I was outside the plane, I reached in to get the passengers out. I hurried to lift each one through the opening in the windshield and onto the ground. By God's grace, we were outside, and able to stand.

"I took a quick look at the airplane and saw the nose had burst open exposing the engine, which lay on the ground sideways. The wing was ripped and the bent propeller faced sideways, also resting on the ground. We rushed away from the plane, but the tribal people were running down the mountain toward the crash site. I yelled, 'Stay back! *Tutubi* could explode.'

"Thankfully, the startled Palawanos heeded the warning. They stopped in their tracks, stared, and shouted, 'Ooo, ooo, ooo, ooo.'

"I didn't realize blood dripped from my face at first. The missionary's wife walked to her *nipa* home to get a cloth to press against my face to slow the bleeding. I needed Doc Joe's help in town, but the only way out of the mountain was to walk and I didn't know the way. Palawano warriors guided me down the winding, eroded path of rocks, mud, and brush and helped me across two shallow rivers. My sprained ankle slowed us down a lot. After several hours, we reached the lowlands. The warriors pointed me to this small village where you and I are currently standing. They turned and hiked back up to their village, leaving me alone.

"I expected someone in the village would help me get back to the base, but no one was home. I looked around again at each hut and on a second look I saw a brand-new blue Kawasaki motorcycle leaning against the hut over there. I hoped it would be my way home."

"It's odd a brand-new motorcycle was in these backwoods."

"The Lord had to be protecting me because the plane crash was only the beginning of a day that went horribly wrong. I started to walk towards the motorcycle when a lone Palawan man strolled out from behind the hut that the cycle leaned against. When I asked if it was his, he said it was. I wanted to borrow it to get home, and to the doctor, but he told me to get on it and he'd take me. A light rain began making the dirt road slippery. Mud, rocks, and dirt flew around and behind us as we zoomed down the back road. We hit potholes and the cycle slid and sputtered. He drove so fast that it made me nervous, especially after surviving a plane crash.

"I yelled, *'Dahan, dahan!'* since the Tagalog word for slow is *dahan*. Instead of slowing down, the motorcycle made a boisterous sound as he revved up the engine to go faster. I held on for dear life with one arm around his waist, and the other holding the cloth against my face. Ahead was a bridge made of thick, uneven railroad ties. They lay side by side, crooked, with gaps between them. There was no way he would be able to drive across it without getting the wheels caught in one of the gaps. I dreaded the crash that was coming. But before we crossed the foreboding bridge, we wrecked."

"You had a motorcycle crash after a plane crash," I said in unbelief.

"We did. The cycle skidded in one direction and the two of us rolled on the rocks in the road in another direction. The man picked up his crashed cycle and pushed it across the bridge with me by his side.

"Most motorcycles didn't have mufflers, but his did and it was torn off when we hit the dirt and slid on the rocks. He climbed back on and with reluctance, I did too. The driver went as fast as possible again. And again, I hollered, *'Dahan, dahan!'* thinking I had told him to slow down. Afterwards, I remembered when you say the word twice, it means, you're going too slowly, so vroom, vroom went the cycle.

"We traveled down the road some more and saw a second rickety bridge had to be crossed. The drop off from this one was even steeper. I felt certain the tires would get caught in the grooves of the bridge's uneven railroad-like ties and we'd fall into the river. I'd survived a plane crash and a motorcycle wreck, but I thought I was going to die on this bridge. But the wobbly cycle lost its balance and fell on the road before we got to the bridge causing even more damage to the motorcycle.

"We climbed back on and to my surprise he got it started and drove straight ahead holding onto handlebars that had been bent sideways. By now, the whole scenario got to be funny, but I wasn't laughing.

"I knew the Lord had to be looking after me. A few more kilometers down the small back road we saw a *jeepney* coming towards us. Although it was going in the opposite direction, I needed its help. I could tell from the position of the sun it would be dark soon. The motorcycle driver stopped to let me off so I could flag it down. I stood in the middle of the road and waved to the driver to stop. I walked up to him and asked that he take me to the flight base, but he hesitated."

"Hesitated. Why?"

"He had a load of passengers who paid to go in the opposite direction and he had to get them home before dark because his vehicle had no headlights. The trip to the flight base and back would take an hour and it would be dark in an hour. But I had to get to the doctor, so he agreed. As he turned the jeepney around, I looked back at the man standing in the middle of the dirt road holding onto the beat-up cycle by its handlebars that sat sideways."

"He'll probably come to the flight base to ask for money to repair his cycle," I remarked.

"Since we are Americans, he'll think we're rich. I may need to buy him a new motorcycle. I don't know if his can be repaired."

We inquired about the Palawano mountain tribe who'd witnessed the plane crash and were told the wreck deeply frightened the tribe. Astonished by what they'd witnessed, about thirty-five of them ran deeper into the jungle to hide because they feared the government would blame them for the crash. The few Christians in the village prayed for their return, and in time, everyone came back.

Rick needed to figure out a way to get the airplane and engine out of the jungle.

Something to Ponder

Apart from God's power and abundant grace the accident would have killed Rick and our friends. The Palawanos witnessed the power of God to save the pilot and family's lives. Just as the prophet Jonah had been delivered from the belly of the big fish, so Rick and his passengers had been delivered from the belly of the crashed airplane. God told Jonah to preach repentance to the people of Nineveh, and Rick's heart was to share truth about God to the tribes. Would they realize from this incident that the power of God is greater than the power of the evil spirits they worship? Would some Palawanos no longer fear retribution from the evil spirits if they turned to Christ because they witnessed His power to deliver? The God of the Bible that Pilot Reeck, as they affectionately called him, and their missionary family worshipped had the power to deliver from certain death. Did theirs?

God is good. But the tribes still in bondage to their religious practices didn't know a loving God. The many gods they worshipped were always going to harm them if they did something to anger the spirits.

Have you seen that God is always good? That He can use a tragedy as an opportunity to reveal Himself? Oh, that men would be freed from the blindness that keeps them caged in their fears. May the Lord open their eyes of understanding to see the love of the true God and trust Him.

Turn our eyes upon Jesus and look full in His wonderful face and we'll never give up when life takes us on an impossible path. "Jesus beheld them, and said unto them, With men this is impossible; but with God all things are possible," (Matthew 19:26)--even walking away from an airplane crash.

Prayer

You, Lord, are great, and greatly to be praised. I worship You in the beauty of Your holiness and bow humbly at Your feet. Thank You that in the womb of the morning sun, I have a new beginning each day to right wrongs and grow in the knowledge of Your glory. May I develop the mind of Christ in humility, love, and obedience. Make my life pleasing in Your sight so I won't be ashamed at Your appearing. Show me the way I am to live and the place I am to go. When I don't understand the twists and turns of life, may I be granted the grace to trust You. I ask that I'll be able to recognize the enemy's fiery darts and quench each one by faith. Strengthen me to complete the purpose for which I was created. For Jesus' name sake I pray. Amen.

CHAPTER FIVE

Putting the Pieces Together

Change was hard for me. I wished things could go back to what I knew as normal.

The airplane and engine still lay in the spot where the plane crashed in the tribal village. Rick searched for someone who could help him carry the Super Cub down the mountain trail but hadn't found anyone yet. The Marines in Brooke's Point told Rick they couldn't help transfer the airplane to the flight base. This task would require manpower since equipment to lift it wasn't available.

Rick would need to carry tools with him on the hike back up to the mountain village so he could separate the airplane into sections before he and other volunteers would be able to carry it down the treacherous forest trail. The tall brush made the path hard for Rick to find his way.

Friends we'd met in Brooke's Point heard about the crash and began to flood our *nipa* home with delicious Philippine dishes. They filled our home with food and cheer from their display of kindness. We always felt somewhat alone living outside of town, but since the plane crash, we'd never felt more integrated with the people.

Meeting the Malacaos

One afternoon we heard someone out front calling *"Taupo, Taupo,"* equivalent to our knock on the door. They introduced themselves as Joe and Fe Malacao, schoolteachers in the area. They had three young boys, Jojo, Jeriel, nicknamed Jay, and Jason. They'd come to pray with us and thank the Lord for sparing our lives in the plane crash.

We welcomed the comfort this couple offered and felt blessed to have someone to pray with us. The spiritual care Joe and Fe offered warmed our hearts and we became instant friends. God put a special bond between us that ended up having an important purpose in future ministry. I hope you'll recognize some of the ways God used this bond as you read the following chapters.

Joe and Fe became regular visitors and we learned more about each other. Years earlier, Joe's parents, as well as Fe's parents had been led to the Lord by missionaries in their home provinces. After Joe graduated from high school, he studied at a Christian mission school in Manila, where he met Fe, a student too. Her big personality filled any space with energy and laughter. Joe, on the other hand, was a man of few words. He admired Fe's outgoing personality, love for the Lord, and intelligence. Fe spoke English well as many in Manila did as it was taught in school.

Believing the Lord put them together, they married and Joe took his new bride home to Brooke's Point, Palawan, one-year shy of graduating. This small detail turned out to be an important factor in the future for good.

A Way Out

On one of the Malacaos' visits to the flight base, Rick let Joe know he needed to find a way to haul the airplane and engine out of the jungle. Not missing a beat, Joe said he could help. Since he taught school in the area close to the path that led to the mountain village. He offered to give his high school boys time out of school to guide Rick to the village and help carry the plane to the lowlands.

Rick was delighted and made plans for Joe's students to meet him at the village where the man with the blue motorcycle had been. The stranger who helped Rick that day hadn't come to the flight base to ask for money to repair his cycle yet, and we still wanted to thank him and pay him for the damages. The morning Rick left to meet the young students he told me he'd check on the man again since he'd be in that same village.

I kissed him good-bye and he left in the jeep pulling the trailer behind it. From the experience Rick had when he hiked out of the jungle, I expected the hike back up to the village to be just as difficult. His ankle seemed like it had healed, or maybe he ignored it.

Much later that day, Rick returned to the flight base with the airplane on the trailer, but I didn't see the engine, the most important part to retrieve. I asked him how things went getting the airplane out of the jungle. He explained that once he arrived at the crash site, he started separating the wings, the engine, the rudder, the elevators, and the landing gear from the fuselage. He had to hurry so they'd have time to carry it down the trail in daylight.

Even in sections, the couple dozen teens and Rick had a hard time carrying the heavy sections of the plane through the thick brush of the jungle. In places, the path they trod was straight down. To avoid falling, they clung to tree branches, shrubs, and the tall grasses because parts of it turned into a gully.

It took several hours before they reached the foothills, but when they did, they placed each section on the trailer. Rick said the students were exhausted and one student declared, "That was hard work."

I asked about the engine and he said it was too heavy for them to carry, so he'd need to go back another time for it. He'd need to find another guide, someone who knew the Palawano dialect. The tribal chieftain agreed to give him four warriors to carry it out.

I remembered he planned to check on the motorcycle driver and asked, "Did you find the man with the blue motorcycle?"

"No, I looked for him, but no one in the village knew him."

The lowlanders told Rick there had never been a new blue motorcycle in the village. Maybe he could find the guy if he asked the auto mechanics since the cycle was damaged and needed repairs.

When in town, he asked auto mechanics about the stranger with the blue motorcycle, but they hadn't seen him. At the same time, he searched for a Palawano guide. Not many people in town could speak Palawano since the main language of the Philippine country was Tagalog.

Rick came home excited because a Palawano man who formerly lived in the mountains said he'd go with him. A couple days later, the two men hiked to the village with the promise from the chieftain of the four warriors to carry the engine to the lowlands.

Rick shared that when the men got to the village of Saray, the atmosphere had changed from the previous visits. The guide and Rick sensed an eerie feeling. His guide told him to wait at the bottom of the village while he checked out the situation with the chieftain, whose nipa hut sat on a hill above the other huts.

As Rick stood below, a tribal woman passed him and cried out, "Oh, no, not you!" She looked frightened. Her presence made the hair stand up on the back of his neck. She hurried away, but when he turned and looked at the feast house, where the tribe worshipped demonic spirits, he froze. Inside was a lady's body floating back and forth in the air. The sight made him feel sick.

Shouting from the guide and chieftain diverted his attention. He realized it had something to do with him when the tribal warriors surrounded him with drawn *bolos*. He was in trouble. Four or five tribal warriors were about to kill him if the chieftain so ordered. He had no idea why. Although his Marine training taught him how to handle this type of situation, he knew he couldn't escape. There were too many to get away from them all. He surrendered to the circumstances, prayed for grace, and committed his life into the Lord's hands.

As he stood there still, Rick became aware that the shouting of the chieftain and the guide lessened and then stopped. After that, the warriors put their *bolos* into their sheaves and walked away.

The guide walked down to where Rick stood to explain what just happened. Some of the fathers of the boys who helped Rick carry *Tutubi* out of the mountain had stolen their white chickens and molested their women. Because of the help the boys gave Rick, the chieftain and warriors assumed Rick was part of the crime, which was punishable by death.

Rick and Joe had no idea some of the boys' fathers had done that to the people and felt horrible that it happened. They knew the people valued the blood of their white chickens to give to the witch doctor as a sacrifice to gain power to avert a curse and heal illnesses. It's only by God's grace that the guide convinced the chieftain otherwise. Rick was surprised to learn the guide still had the courage to ask the chieftain if he would provide warriors to carry out the engine, but he did, and the chieftain agreed.

Rick noticed the chieftain looking at the sun through a piece of broken, green Plexiglas from the crashed airplane. He told the chieftain he could keep it and it made him happy.

Rick watched the warriors prepare to haul the engine. They cut down two bamboo poles from the jungle and used vines to tie the poles together in the shape of an X. The warriors wrapped the engine around and around with vines, then tied the vine with the engine to the center of the poles. Super Cub engines weighed between three hundred and three hundred and eighty pounds. The average warrior's height was just five feet.

Four warriors positioned the bamboo carrier on their shoulders and lifted the heavy engine. When Rick tried to help lift it, his height drove the weight into the two Palawanos' shoulders on the opposite end, so he wasn't helpful.

I imagined the bare, calloused, thick-skinned feet of the warriors gripping the slippery dirt path on the downhill track. I remembered their swollen toes spread apart wider than their feet. Daily they hiked, hunted, and climbed trees barefoot.

When the warriors arrived at places on the trail where they could see a shallow river below, they untied the engine and let it roll downhill. It bounced and tumbled into the waist-deep water with a big splash. The Palawanos rolled on the ground in laughter, and enjoyed a break from the weight they carried. Rick smiled and welcomed their laughter. It was a relief from the angry faces and threatening *bolos* he faced a few hours earlier.

When they reached the small village in the lowland, the tribesmen placed the engine on the trailer, relieved. Rick rewarded them with pesos, but they looked at him as if to say, *what are we supposed to do with this money? We can't eat it.* However, they graciously accepted, then trotted back to their village. They could run like cheetahs through the dense forest.

Thirty-four years would pass before I'd meet these people to thank them, or before Rick would see them again. Some would die in the meantime, but we had a grand reunion when we saw some of them again, but that's for another chapter.

With the airplane and engine at the base, Rick built a crate, put them inside, took the crate to the pier, and shipped them to the flight base north of Manila for overhaul.

I asked him again if he found the man who owned the blue motorcycle since he was back in that village.

"Not yet," and he proceeded to tell me what he found.

The Stranger with the Blue Motorcycle

Rick asked the lowlanders one more time if they'd seen the man with the blue motorcycle. He pointed to the hut it leaned up against, thinking the people in that hut might know who he was. Although everyone had heard about the plane crash, no one knew about this man and hadn't seen a new, blue motorcycle, or a crashed one. In fact, the people told Rick, "Sir, there has never been a new blue motorcycle in this village. The man you say was here, we've never seen."

We thought it strange the man hadn't shown up at the base to ask for payment. The mechanics Rick checked with on the island hadn't seen anyone come in with a damaged blue motorcycle with bent handlebars. On a small island everyone knew each other making it obvious if a stranger was around. We recalled how strange it was that not one person had been in the village that late afternoon when Rick came out of the mountain, except this lone man. Someone should have seen a wrecked blue Kawasaki motorcycle in the area, but they hadn't.

Did God send an angel to rescue Rick? It remains a mystery to this day.

Something to Ponder

The Super Cub was in pieces and my life felt like it was in pieces too, pieces that didn't fit together in a neat, clear picture. God's purpose for Rick, as we understood it had been to provide air support to the missionaries in the jungles. Without the airplane, he couldn't do that.

Have you experienced situations when your life with God feels like pieces of a puzzle you can't fit together? Do you wish like I have that you could figure it out and see the whole picture? I'm convinced that living by faith means we only see parts of the puzzle, a little at a time, until the whole picture is known one day in glory.

Because we know who made us, we know who formed each part of the puzzle that unfolds in our lives. Therefore, we know the pieces do fit together to complete God's perfect plan.

I believe God can be trusted and will guide us through each part of life's challenges, one step at a time. We see parts of His plan now by looking back and seeing the good that came from each pain, each loss, and each illness. But when we're with Him in heaven, we will see the whole of our lives as God sees them and rejoice greatly in His goodness, mercy, and love.

Serve Him today with a heart of passion for Him and His people. It is worth it all. "For I know the thoughts that I think toward you, saith the Lord, thoughts of peace, and not of evil, to give you an expected end." (Jeremiah 29:11)

Prayer

How can I thank You, Lord, for the personal ways You pay attention to me and my life? You are always with me to guide me in the way I should go. Your Word is a lamp unto my feet and a light unto my path. My goings are in Your hands. Thank You for Your personal care of my life and those I love. Your amazing grace sustains me and Your mercy upholds me that life's challenges don't overtake me. You provide a way for Your children to prosper and find victory in all our affairs. A crisis in our life is no problem for You. Courage and strength are given to us in the portions needed that we might overcome our struggles and accomplish Your will. You are the Divine Creator, the Supreme One who is love. I rest in the knowledge of my eternal, unchanging God. In Jesus' name I pray. Amen.

CHAPTER SIX

The Question That Changed Everything

"Taupo." A second call came from the front of our house. We went to the bamboo porch to see who was there. Joe and Fe stood at the bottom of our porch stairs. Our relationship had strengthened as we became better acquainted with each other. They had the same desire as we did, to see all people of southern Palawan reached with the love of Jesus Christ.

Rick shared with them about seeing little villages of huts scattered throughout the forest on his flights, especially on the west side of the island. They had no path going in or out of their villages, which signaled to him that no one had been there with the gospel. Hiking to their villages looked impossible due to the terrain. An airplane, even a helicopter was out of the question in the web below him. Joe said he'd also heard of unreached people who lived in a cave somewhere in the highlands.

Joe longed to see a new local church established in Brooke's Point that taught the whole council of God. He wanted his people to know what pleased and displeased the Lord. It seemed to me there was a lack of a general knowledge of the God of the Bible. That's understandable when many, even most, didn't own a copy of God's Word. It wasn't even sold on the island. Those who had a copy bought theirs in Manila. I wasn't used to seeing a picture of a loosely dressed woman on a businessman's wall with a picture of Jesus beside it.

People in the mountains especially needed to hear the Word. They were kept under bondage to religious practices passed down to them by their ancestors. Joe believed the truth of Scripture could set them free from their paganistic worship, and we agreed. I witnessed how a way of life developed over centuries not based on the foundation of the Bible.

Because Joe and Fe were poor, they held no influence or say in the town at the time, but they possessed a God-given burden for their people. Our conversation ended up with Joe asking Rick and me an unexpected question. "Will you and Carolyn pray about helping us start a Bible-preaching church in town? If you are willing, we will surely be your partners."

Church planting seemed so far removed from anything we'd consider that we didn't take the request seriously. Rick commented to Joe that he didn't believe he qualified to be a church planter since he trained to be a jungle pilot.

But Joe appealed to him. "Will you pray about it?"

How can you tell someone you're not willing to pray about something? Rick agreed to pray about starting a church with Joe but never expected anything to come of it. I put Joe's question out of my mind thinking that would never happen. The thought of change bothered me, but the Scriptures brought me comfort.

We left for the States on furlough thinking that would be the end of the matter.

When we arrived in the States, a few friends from our home church had a little white house in the country ready for us. It was the perfect place to regroup and prepare for future ministry. Rick traveled to supporting churches to update them and thanked them for their support. I often stayed behind with the children since they had school.

I'd forgotten how busy and full people's lives were in the States. Living on a remote island, I'd gotten accustomed to a slower pace of life and liked it. At the end of the day I felt like I'd lived each hour of it rather than it going by in a blur.

I hoped my closest friends would have time for me. My heart was full and I wanted to tell them about my foreign experiences. When I did try to express myself, I don't think they could identify. I'd heard it was harder for missionaries to readjust to American culture than to the new culture of a foreign country. It's true in part because one becomes a mixture of two cultures when living abroad. It's easy to make unintended social blunders when back in the States. Overseas you can be excused as a foreigner, but not in the States.

Letters from Joe and Fe became a special treat. Joe's resolve that we pray about helping them start a new church in Brooke's Point became like the man in Paul's vision in the Book of Acts. This man appeared to Paul and asked that he go into Macedonia and help them. That's what Joe and Fe's pleas became to us.

The Malacaos knew Rick planned to remain in aviation. He'd made that clear to Joe. After all the time and money we had poured into aviation training, it didn't seem likely to us that Rick would be redirected into church planting.

He wrote Joe a letter and told him again he wasn't a church planter but a missionary pilot. Joe wrote back and said to continue to pray about it. Rick kept his promise and prayed for God's will rather than assume he already knew it. I prayed he'd have clarity.

Rick and I began to discuss his main reason for

not going into church planting—he didn't feel qualified. We remembered the missionary training we'd received, which was identical to the practical training the missionaries working with the tribes had. We were in classes with them. Good practical training had prepared us well.

A Unique Preparation

Each morning our training began with classes until noon. In one session each missionary candidate was required to *practice giving the gospel*. The instructors divided us into pairs and gave us two minutes to present the gospel to our partner. The mission believed if we could share the gospel in two minutes, we knew it well.

Afterwards, we critiqued each one's presentation by stating what we felt was good and what, if anything, could make it clearer. Then we went into the community to share the good news of Jesus Christ with strangers.

In another class, we were required to *write doctrinal papers using only our memory as the source.*

Each of us had thirty minutes to write a paper that explained our understanding of the assigned doctrine. It had to be written on a fourth-grade level without looking up Scripture verses, but we could use the ones we'd put to memory. The mission wasn't looking for us to wax elegant, but they needed to know if we knew what we believed and could share it with others in a comprehensive way.

I found the training on *how to determine a tribe's culture* most interesting.

From listening to recorded dialogue of a tribe, I learned to determine what the people believed about God, life, and death. I could even uncover their value system and customs. This exercise taught the candidates to assess a people's way of life. Once we learned their customs and beliefs, we could compare what they believed with the truth of Scripture. Unbiblical beliefs could be countered with truth. Witnessing became more effective as we came to understand the way people thought. We'd rely on the Spirit of God to help them receive truth presented.

Learning how life worked for the people helped me better see the reason behind some behaviors, which could seem strange to us, but our customs can be just as strange to them. When we're able to understand the people's way of life, we're less likely to offend them. To see others possess saving faith through the Lord Jesus Christ was my purpose for leaving my home and country. Therefore, I valued this exercise and learned much from it.

As candidates our ability to work as a team was tested through afternoon sports. How well we could trust God in the unknowns was tried by being placed in situations unfamiliar to us like killing a chicken and shooting a rifle for me.

Our past training experiences became instrumental in determining God's leading about planting a church with Joe and Fe. It would take a great deal of faith to do such a thing. But we came to realize, our practical training had been in church planting as well as aviation.

As Rick sought the mind of the Lord about Joe's request, I meditated on Proverbs 3:6, "In all thy ways acknowledge him, and he shall direct thy paths," and saw paths in this verse is plural. God may take His people on different paths to fulfill His purpose for their life. As we walk by faith, the paths God wants us to tread disclose a little each day until we know what to do. If helping Joe plant a church was of God, it would come to pass.

This verse became a prayer of my heart. "Cause me (and Rick) to know the way wherein I should walk; for I lift up my soul unto thee." (Psalm 143:8)

As Rick prayed, his mind remembered the scattered tribes he'd seen in the mountains on flights, separated from civilization. He felt burdened to reach them with the gospel. He believed God wanted to make Himself known to these people, but it seemed impossible.

Accepting Change

It troubled me to think about not serving the missionaries with the airplane that they relied on. I believed the work we had done was important and made a difference in the lives of the people. The Lord reminded me that the missionaries were His people and I could trust Him to take care of them. My responsibility was to obey His leading for my life, whatever that would be. A principle in Scripture from 1 Samuel 15 spoke to my heart.

In the Old Testament the Amalekites cruelly attacked Israel for no reason during a vulnerable time in their history. Samuel gave King Saul precise instructions from the Lord that he and his army were to destroy all of the Amalekites and all their possessions because of the wrong done to His people.

However, King Saul chose to destroy *most* of the Amalekites and a large portion of all they had. But *most* is not all. He spared King Agag and kept the best of their sheep and oxen.

Grieving Samuel approached Saul. When he saw Samuel coming, he greeted him with these words, "Blessed be thou of the Lord: I have performed the commandment of the Lord." (1 Samuel 15:13)

But had he?

I questioned myself. Did I ever convince myself I had obeyed God when I only partially obeyed? The command God gave to Saul was not an easy one to follow, but God's Spirit would have given him the grace to obey all the Lord required of him. The king made an excuse for his disobedience. He told Samuel he planned to use the sheep and oxen as sacrifices to the Lord.

As Saul justified his disobedience, I wrestled in my spirit about the good our aviation ministry accomplished. We had served the Lord in the way He led us. What would it hurt to continue? But I read further.

Samuel was not impressed by Saul's reason to obey the Lord in part and said, "What meaneth then this bleating of the sheep in mine ears, and the lowing of the oxen which I hear?" King Saul had sinned against God's command to destroy all, and the Bible says it was "evil in the sight of the Lord." (1 Samuel 15:19)

First Samuel 15:22 says, "Hath the Lord as great delight in burnt offerings and sacrifices, as in obeying the voice of the Lord? Behold, to obey is better than sacrifice, and to hearken than the fat of rams."

I saw that the Lord values obedience to Him more than service for Him. All the good works in the ministry of aviation would be eternally meaningless going forward unless the Lord wanted Rick and me to continue to serve in this capacity. I began to entertain the idea of Rick becoming a church planter without fretting over the people or past joys of the ministry. I'd do as the Lord led.

Rick's excuse that he wasn't a church planter no longer held. Not only had we been trained to take the gospel to people in remote places, but we had the message, God's Word, and the guidance and empowerment of the Holy Spirit. With these tools, we could accomplish whatever the Lord wanted us to do. "For it is God which worketh in you both to will and to do of his good pleasure." (Philippians 2:13)

In time, Rick came to me and said, "As much as I loved flying as a missionary pilot, leading souls to Christ and organizing them into a local church excites me more."

I wasn't surprised.

He shared a verse from Proverbs 29:18: "Where there is no vision, the people perish." He studied the word vision in the passage and discovered it meant a revelation, a sight seen with the mind. To have vision is to have spiritual understanding concerning the Word of God. It became clear to him that he was to be one of God's messengers to impart to the people of southern Palawan a spiritual understanding regarding Jesus Christ.

Rick and I met with our pastor to discuss going back to Palawan to start a local church for the people. Pastor Dale quizzed me. "Do you want to go back and work with Joe and Fe to plant a church?"

I heard a resounding "Yes" come from the depths of my soul. God had done a work in my heart and it no longer mattered if He changed our ministry from aviation to church planting, only that we knew His mind and obeyed His will. Our pastor commented that he had peace about this change too.

I knew misunderstandings would arise as a result of Rick's decision, but we'd go through the doors God opened. If He shut the door to this, we would not beat it down for we can do nothing without Him.

I wondered about our three children. How would they feel about a change? When Rick asked them about going back to Palawan to help Joe plant a church, I smiled at their reaction. Without any reluctance Scott and Brad jumped up and down with glee and said, "Yes." Angie watched their cheerfulness and clapped her little hands.

Before our final decision, Rick took a survey trip to Palawan to meet with Joe and Fe. Almost the same day Rick decided to make the trip, money was given for plane fare. When he returned from the survey, he said it confirmed to him that the Lord wanted us to help start a church in Brooke's Point. "This is the way, walk ye in it." (Isaiah 30:21)

A great and effectual door had been opened and according to Revelation 3:8, when God opens a door, "no man can shut it." As we went forward, obstacles were removed and it seemed like doors not only opened but flew open. Because of God's faithfulness in the past to make the impossible possible, we knew one day there would be a new church in Brooke's Point, Palawan.

Rick mailed a very welcomed letter to Joe to let him know we'd help them start a church. Their prayers had been answered. Although change was difficult for me, the Lord had prepared my heart to accept this change with joy. The Malacaos had news for us too. God had blessed them with another son they named Jethro (Jeth).

Mentoring

Since Rick believed he'd been redirected of the Lord to plant a church with Joe, the unmistakable leading of the Holy Spirit sustained me. God would be faithful to keep me faithful to His call just as He'd promised so many years earlier.

Pastor McCallister met with Rick the next few months and methodically taught him local church government. He learned what a local church was, what it looked like, and how to know when it qualified as a local New Testament church according to the Scriptures. They also studied the universal church. He finished courses online to complete his theology degree.

As Rick studied with our pastor, they agreed the most effective way to reach the unreached tribes in the mountains was to begin with a church in Brooke's Point. Joe and Rick could train the people in the congregation to reach their own as the church became established. The Palawan people better understood the culture and the language and could manage the difficult living conditions in the mountains more readily than a foreign missionary.

Furlough ended and our family was eager to get back on the field. Rick felt equipped to teach Joe principles of church planting. We didn't expect the work to be easy but had no idea how much adversity lay ahead.

Something to Ponder

Being open to whatever the Lord has for our life can take us on an alternate journey from the one we planned. It's a future out of our control. Are we okay with that? I've learned that doing whatever God leads me to do may take rough turns but ends with joyful blessings. When I rely on what I think makes more sense, or what I want, the result is a toss-up between a mediocre life to frustration—even failure. I want more for my Christian life than just getting by. I want one that flourishes, prospers, and is fulfilling.

If we worry about what someone else will think about a decision we need to make, we can lose the blessing God has for us that comes through obedience. The key is to know it is He who leads us in the choices we make, for the outcome of our lives becomes a result of the decisions we've made.

We don't need to understand why God directs us as He does, but it is important to trust Him. What has God put in your heart to do? Do it with all your might by His grace for His glory and rejoice for it holds eternal worth. "A man's heart deviseth his way: but the LORD directeth his steps." (Proverbs 16:9)

Prayer

Heavenly Father, You are the one who guides me by Your Word and prayer, arranging circumstances to bring me to a place where I can clearly see my next step with You. You give me the grace to obey Your will and then bless my obedience in manifold ways. All of it, the grace to obey and the blessings that follow is all of You.

I'm glad You don't hide the path of life You want me to take, but make it clear that I can have confidence in my walk with You. Thank You for having me in Your thoughts. Because I know Your Word is truth, I will trust my future to Your keeping, knowing You have a purpose in all You allow in my life. Help me stay close to You that I not be deceived by the devil's devices and fall short of a full blessing on that glorious day in heaven. May I always give You my best in loving service. Thank You for the privilege of being Your child. In Your Son's name I pray. Amen.

CHAPTER SEVEN

Everything's Backwards

Broad smiles covered our faces as Rick and I sat aboard a 747 jet with our three children headed back to Manila, Philippines. As the jet's wheels lifted off the ground, our hearts were full of anticipation and sheer excitement. We were embarking on a new adventure with purpose and direction. Twenty-four hours later, we arrived in Manila and stayed with friends.

We walked around the neighborhood to look for a house to rent and found one in the clean, safe section of BF Homes. The homes were gated and the windows barred for protection. We planned to live in the Manila area a year to study the Tagalog language before moving to Palawan. It hadn't occurred to us that the cost of living would be as expensive as it was. Our support would be stretched to pay the rent, but we didn't know where else to go.

In the providence of God, Joe and Fe also moved to the Manila island so he could finish his last year of Bible school. They visited us with their four sons from Cavite, a four-hour trip by public transportation. I was overjoyed to see them again and meet their new son, Jeth. Rick and Joe seized the opportunity of having a year together and decided to hold weekly Bible studies at Joe's home. As Rick learned Tagalog and Joe finished his degree, they studied the local church and planned a strategy for starting a new one in Brooke's Point.

Adjustments to a New Way of Life

Christmas was approaching and I wanted a tree for the children to enjoy, but pine trees didn't grow there. Resourceful Fe helped me make a tree out of strands of green crepe paper. We taped the strands to the ceiling, then twirled each strand as we pulled it out from the corner of the wall and taped it to the parquet floors. An advantage of being financially challenged was that it taught us and our children to be creative. A board game and a doll for Angie were gifts under our crepe paper tree. The boys wrapped one of their Matchbox cars and gave them to each other. It satisfied us, and a Christmas dinner with Joe and Fe and other missionaries brought sweet fellowship to our home.

Some things were not hard to adjust to, like new friendships that developed, scrumptious fruits, warm weather, palm trees, and the ocean. However, others were a challenge.

Culture shock has been described by some as everything you do, or think, seems backwards from what is natural to you. I felt disoriented at times in our new country. The sights, sounds, and smells were different. The food, climate, and language were different. Traffic, vehicles, and methods of travel were different. Medical care, illnesses, and treatments were different. I felt like a two-year-old as I learned to speak Tagalog, think as Filipinos do, and live in my new world.

Life felt irritating and confusing, even haywire at times. Two different people claimed to own the house we were renting, both demanding payments. An attitude of some was *what does it hurt a rich American to pay twice.* Compared to their poor, I was rich.

The rudeness of the doctor I took Brad to perplexed me. He rudely said, "Brad has enlarged adenoids that he'll outgrow. Don't bring him back here again."

What? Why? I felt slapped in the face. Brad had trouble swallowing and breathing.

Rick took Scott to the dentist, and when they came home, the dentist had removed the retainer on his bottom teeth and pulled an upper front side tooth to make room for the new tooth coming in. I groaned.

Another time, the eye doctor told us that Scott needed glasses. Of course, we bought him glasses. Later we found out he didn't need them. The people referred to this as getting fooled. It was our responsibility to be smart enough not to get tricked.

I traveled by *tricycle* to the open market to buy groceries. As many as nineteen Philippine people could pile onto one *tricycle*, which held about six Philippine people, or four Americans.

I walked from vendor to vendor making purchases and bartering for the best price on meat, vegetables, and fruit. My plastic bags were heavy and cut into my palms and fingers, causing my hands to be red and swollen.

One of the vendors saw my bright red, puffy hands and asked me, "Where is your car?"

"I don't own a car."

"Why not?"

"We don't have money to purchase one."

She sarcastically spewed, "I don't know why you don't have a car, but I know it's not because you don't have money."

She frustrated me. I wasn't carrying those bags for pleasure. It took years for me not to recoil anytime someone handed me a plastic bag.

Traveling in public transportation made me ill from the fumes of a multitude of *jeepneys* without mufflers. It startled me one afternoon when a peddler jumped inside the back of the public *jeepney* I was on to sell passengers a piece of candy, a newspaper, or a single cigarette. The items were on a wooden tray that hung from his neck with a wide strap.

Rick and I were delighted when a supporting church in Ohio gave us permission to use funds designated to build a *nipa* house on Palawan to purchase a much-needed vehicle. Now travel to Joe's took two hours instead of four. I stayed behind to teach school to our boys and care for Angie. The children were our priority.

Driving in traffic in place of riding in it required additional patience as vehicles crisscrossed and appeared like a herd of cattle trying to get through one gate at the same time. No one stayed in their own lane. Whoever could squeeze the front end of their automobile between you and the jeep in front of you had the right of way. Rick assured me there was a system to the madness, if you could figure it out.

He learned the hard way how to make a left turn when driving. He had stuck his arm out the window and his left turn signal blinked to be sure the traffic behind him knew he was turning left. When he made the turn, somehow the car behind us ended up in front of us with our car still sideways across the lane of traffic. Did they go through us? Startled, Rick and I gazed at the other car and saw the angry faces of the people in it. We didn't realize that traffic behind us had the right-of-way. Bewildered, the next time we'd know to let the cars behind us pass us before we turned.

The grass in our yard needed cut, but homeowners didn't have lawnmowers. We couldn't squat for hours in the hot sun and cut grass with hand sheers like Filipino men did. Many Filipinos couldn't do it either, so a grasscutter was hired.

One morning the man we hired came to the back door in the middle of his work and asked, "May I take a shower?"

That seemed strange. "You're asking if you can shower in our bathroom—now?"

"Yes," he answered like it was the most normal thing in the world.

"Are you finished with your work?"

"No."

I didn't understand why he'd shower before his work was done, and I didn't feel comfortable having a man I didn't know take a shower in our house. However, I told him he could use our shower when he finished his work.

Highly offended, he looked crossly at me. "I don't want to die!" he mumbled as he walked away.

Die. What was he talking about?

I found out he told people that I was mean. It crushed me that he thought that. I didn't want that reputation when we were trying to share God's love with them.

Confused by his comments, the next time Joe and Fe visited, I explained what happened. Fe informed us that in the tropical climate, they shower when they feel overheated to prevent a heat-stroke.

Oh, now I understood. His unreasonable request became very reasonable. I'd be sure to tell him he could use the shower whenever he needed it. I also wanted to tell him I was sorry, but he never returned.

Learning the Filipino culture was an ongoing process. The people shared their belongings with others as a common practice. Rick let a friend from church borrow his hammer, but he never returned it. He asked Fe why the man hadn't brought his hammer back.

She innocently asked, "Do you need it?"

"Not right now."

"When you need it, you can ask for it back. He'll give it to you."

I learned that just because something isn't done the way it's done in America doesn't make it wrong— just different.

Rick was excited for the opportunity to speak at a small church to practice preaching in the Tagalog language. He wrote out his message and Joe went with him for support.

When Rick came home, he walked inside with his head down, feeling deflated. Two girls in the front row laughed through his entire message. We were advised to work on our diction and vowel pronunciations for people to better understand us.

The next chance Rick got to preach in Tagalog, our whole family went as did the entire Malacao family. When Rick introduced Joe and Fe to the congregation, he meant to say, "They are small in stature, but have big hearts for the Lord." Instead he said, "They are small people, but have big cats." The word for cat is *pusa*, and the word for heart is *puso*. It's no wonder people laughed. We laughed, too. Learning to speak another language required humility. We accepted the fact we'd be laughed at and kept on trying. Our children picked up the language with ease and no American accent.

Fe's parents invited our family to visit their home. We looked forward to meeting them. After everyone greeted each other, Fe's father asked Rick how we got to his place. Rick pointed to his Isuzu vehicle parked outside and said in Tagalog, "I drove here in my *Isuzu*."

Fe's father became infuriated and muttered words we couldn't understand, then abruptly left the room. Rick wondered what he said to provoke Fe's father.

She went to him in the kitchen. "*Tatay*, why are you upset with Pastor Searls?"

"How can he call himself a missionary and speak to me as he did?"

"What do you think he said?"

"When I asked how he got here, he told me to go nurse like a baby with its mother."

Fe laughed until tears rolled down her cheeks. "*Tatay*, Rick is saying *Isuzu*. He drove us here in his *Isuzu* jeep. Look," and pointed outside to it. A similar Tagalog word means to nurse.

Her father went from being ready to disown Rick to being amused. She had a lot of examples of mispronunciations she could cite to convince him Rick didn't mean to say the other word. We still laugh today at that one.

I had one Tagalog word down—*Talaga*. In English it could mean, *Really,* with a period, or *Really?* and the big one—*Really!* People asked if I knew any other word. I laughed. It was time for me to expand my vocabulary.

To accomplish what God gave us to do for His glory, we couldn't take offense at the many ways the people offended us. We put cultural differences aside, even when misunderstandings caused hurt, for the cause of Christ. We hoped they'd do the same for us. Good communication helped everyone understand the meaning behind comments and behaviors. Fe came along side us in major ways to keep the peace as we blundered our way through the process of cultural adjustments.

Rick and Joe's Studies

Rick and Joe's time together to pray for the work on Palawan, study the local church, and strategize for its development proved to be a tremendous advantage for the work on Palawan and grew their relationship. Although backgrounds and cultures were different, we were one in Christ, in the call of God upon our lives, and united for the souls of people in southern Palawan. As Rick taught the purpose of the local church, Joe taught Rick about the customs and beliefs of the Palawan people.

The men examined the call of God on Barnabas and Saul in the Book of Acts. "As they ministered to the Lord, and fasted, the Holy Ghost said, Separate me Barnabas and Saul for the work whereunto I have called them." (Acts 13:2) "So they, being sent forth by the Holy Ghost, departed." (Acts 13:4) God called faithful men who were active in the local church.

Just as the Holy Spirit sent Barnabas and Paul out into His harvest field, Rick and Joe, along with Fe and me, believed the Holy Spirit had separated us for the harvest field of southern Palawan.

Rick showed us a verse with a simplistic view of a functioning local church. "Paul and Timotheus, the servants of Jesus Christ, to all the saints in Christ Jesus which are at Philippi, with the bishops and deacons." (Philippians 1:1) In the verse, the local church consisted of a group of believers in Christ in a local area with bishops, or pastors/elders, and deacons. Rick emphasized that "Christ is the head of the church" (Ephesians 5:23) and leadership must follow and hold to its head.

They studied the qualifications of local church leaders out of 1 Timothy 3 so they'd be able to spot leaders among the church family. Rick also instructed Joe in the mission of the local church.

1. Evangelize the local area according to Acts 1:8, and the world in obedience to the great commission given in Matthew 28:18-20.
2. Guard the truth, such as Christ's deity, righteousness, love, salvation, eternal life, and all the doctrines and Bible truths. 1

Timothy 3:15; John 14:6; and 2 Timothy 2:1-2

3. Edify the saints as seen in Ephesians 4:11-16, declaring the whole counsel of God. Acts 20:27

Rick and Joe agreed they'd teach the mission of the church to the congregation God gave them. In addition, three qualifications for the church would determine when it was ready to operate under all Philippine leadership:

1. Self-governing - *Has its own qualified leadership, apt to teach*
2. Self-supporting - *Able to pay its own expenses*
3. Self-propagating - *Self-witnessing—reproducing itself*

These last three would be the long-term goals for the local church, while always maintaining its mission. We had our blueprint to keep us focused.

A spiritually strong church in Brooke's Point was the first step the four of us wanted to accomplish. Sound doctrine was key. We decided to call the church Brooke's Point Bible Church (BPBC) because Brooke's Point was the locality; we taught the Bible, and we planned to establish a church. It would unlock the door of opportunity to reach beyond Brooke's Point to the barrios and mountains with the gospel to start more churches.

The men prayed that their vision of saturating southern Palawan with the gospel would be caught by the future congregation of the church. They anticipated discipling new believers, training them, and then sending them forth in the Lord's harvest field.

Palawan Bound

The year in Manila went fast. Joe completed his studies in September of 1982, and Rick and I graduated from language school around the same time. Before leaving for Palawan, Rick told me he needed to spend the night in prayer for our future ministry with Joe and Fe.

When the sun rose the next morning, he came to me with peace that the Lord had confirmed to him that he was to go to Palawan with Joe and Fe as our coworkers, live with them, cry with them, laugh with them, teach them what he knew, and then leave.

"Leave?" I questioned.

"Yes."

That meant we wouldn't be spending our entire ministry in Brooke's Point. It gave me mixed feelings, but I'd concentrate on the living, crying, and laughing part now and support my husband.

Since Joe, Fe, Rick and I knew the Lord made us ministry partners, Pastor Joe later said with a wink and a smile, "What God hath joined together, let not man put asunder." Joe knew that passage from Mark 10 referred to a husband and wife relationship, but he used the verse to make a point about our relationship. In my opinion, the principle was a good one and necessary to consider as future attacks and misunderstandings would come into play.

Before Joe left for Palawan, his professor offered him a teaching position at the Bible school. Joe turned him down. The professor was concerned for Joe's safety going to Brooke's Point to start another church as there was strong opposition from those opposed to a new church in town. Then Joe was offered money to work with a certain mission group, but he declined. A third offer came from another mission board with a promise of financial support, and he said no thank you to them as well.

All these offers would have made their lives much easier. They didn't have any support at the time and we didn't have enough support to pay them. The four of us looked to the Lord to take care of us and went forward with unshakeable faith that planting a new church in Brooke's Point was what the Lord wanted us to do.

When Joe and Fe weren't persuaded with money or position, a few people made fun of them and said there was no way they could start a church in town. Someone called them boastful and another, liars. Others believed they would never make it without their teaching jobs and would come crawling back for help. But ridicule didn't stop them either.

They received a threat from one man on the island that he'd behead them if they followed through with their plans. Joe and Fe kept this piece of information from Rick and me for years fearing we'd not help them if we knew the possible dangers. But nothing could prevent either of our families from starting the church since we were convinced it was God's will. We feared disobeying God more than financial struggles, ridicule, or empty threats of men.

Accusations came against us to Joe and Fe, and against Joe and Fe to us. The gossip didn't discourage us but reminded us of Sanballat, Tobiah, and Geshem in the Book of Nehemiah. These men used slander to try to stop the Israelites from building the wall around Jerusalem. "Then I [Nehemiah] sent unto him [Sanballat], saying, There are no such things done as thou sayest, but thou feignest them out of thine own heart." (Nehemiah 6:8) Nehemiah led his people in building the wall and saw its completion. We believed the *wall* God wanted us to build would be built by His grace. "Above all, taking the shield of faith, wherewith ye shall be able to quench all the fiery darts of the wicked *one*." (Ephesians 6:16)

The last time our family had been on Palawan was after the plane crash, two-and-a-half years ago. Excitement filled my heart to set foot on the island again. Even in the baking heat, it felt like home.

Joe and Fe's welcoming faces greeted us at the little airport in the capital city of Puerto Princesa. They arrived on the island the previous week. We rested overnight before the dusty ride south to Brooke's Point on an old rusty bus. The travel time would take seven hours, provided there were no flat tires or breakdowns, which happened regularly.

Before leaving the next morning, Fe prepared a breakfast of hamburgers and mangoes. Since there were no meat grinders, I knew she had to chop the meat in fine pieces by hand. She once cooked for American missionaries in Manila and knew we liked hamburgers.

Rick, the children, and I had never eaten mangoes and didn't know what they were. The taste was strange at first, but good. Fe stared at Rick dumbfounded watching as he ate the rind of the mango and asked, "Do Americans eat the rinds too?" When he explained he ate it because he didn't want to offend them, everyone erupted in laughter.

We took a *tricycle* to the bus station and stepped over holes in the floorboard boarding the bus. We sat on small wooden, slatted, bench-like seats. I held onto Angie to keep her from being tossed around and falling onto the floor. Behind us freshly caught fish hung on a string, carrying a strong odor. There was no glass in the windows, so dust flooded the bus and covered our faces like paint.

I watched Rick turn his head to see a squealing pig in the aisle, just as a chicken flapped its wings and caused him to lean backwards to avoid getting hit in the face by it. Folks stood in the aisle, straddling the holes to prevent their foot from falling through the floor. The lone road we traveled was full of potholes, twists and turns, up hills and through creeks where the bridges were out. Fumes from the bus, the smell of fish, coupled with twists and turns to avoid potholes made the journey a nauseating experience.

When the bus stopped along the side of the road for a break, I started to get off to stretch my legs. But the panicked faces of people looked at me and blocked my exit by sticking their legs and arms in my path. One of the passengers explained why.

I asked her. "Why would the men relieve themselves in front of ladies?" She replied in a matter of fact way. "The lady is expected to turn her head."

I took my seat.

The temporary stop ended and as we drove off, I leaned back and enjoyed watching a farmer guide a *carabao* as it plowed through the wet rice field. A cloth covered his head and his feet sunk into the muddy ground as the *carabao* took each step forward. *How do the people endure working in the tropical heat? How will I?*

My mind was alerted to danger as the bus driver rounded a sharp curve along a dangerous drop-off. I prayed. If the bus slid in the gravel on the dirt road, there were no guard rails to protect it from tumbling off the cliff. Why didn't he slow down? I would soon find out part of it had to do with his belief system. The Palawan people have a saying, "Bahala Na." In English it can be translated, "Come what may," a fatalistic view of life. If the bus had an accident, it was destiny, not his driving. He knew little about personal responsibility.

Natural laws were either being ignored or not understood. If the Lord wanted Rick and me to proclaim the gospel to these people, He needed to protect us on the bus ride. Since we believed He did want us to proclaim Christ to the people, I felt safe.

As dust flew and the wind blew on my face, I looked up at the blue skies decorated with white, fluffy clouds. They were the one thing that looked familiar to me. As I talked to the Lord, He impressed upon my heart not to fear anything we would encounter in Brooke's Point because He had many people in this place. I remembered He had spoken similar words to Paul. "I am with thee, and no man shall set on thee to hurt thee: for I have much people in this city." (Acts 18:10) From this I was given courage that I didn't know I would need. The excitement of starting our church kept me from thinking about adversity.

Something to Ponder

Piloting our way through a new culture and learning how to adjust in a new environment is a constant in life. People are different even within the same country. What helped through our adjustments was to think of the reason to endure it—that we could reach the lost with the gospel of Christ. Christ's love constrains us wherever we are.

In the providence of God, plans come together to assist us so we can succeed at the work He wants us to do. He puts people and events together to bring about His plan for us and directs us along the path we're to walk. Accept support from others who have gone through similar experiences and pray together. Ask questions. Gather information. Then depend on the wisdom needed to be yours through Christ. "Be strong and of good courage, fear not, nor be afraid of them: for the Lord thy God, he it is that doth go with thee; he will not fail thee, nor forsake thee." (Deuteronomy 31:6) We don't need to fear what we don't understand, only fear Him.

Prayer

Lord, help me accept new situations that I may be at peace. Remind me that You are with me, therefore, there's no need to fear. Let me take courage because You will never fail me. Help me learn to be content as I rest upon Christ, not my circumstances. When life around me is confusing and irritating, cause me to look to You, my constant companion, foundation, and rock. When misunderstandings, trials, and temptations are hurled my way, hold my hand to keep me standing that I not fail Thee. Cause me to cease striving, but "be still and know that Thou art God." (Psalm 46:10) For Jesus' name sake I pray. Amen.

CHAPTER EIGHT

A Church Is Born

We arrived in Brooke's Point covered in dust and worn out from the rugged bus trip. Life there was so much more difficult, no matter what you did. We needed showers but had no place to live. A boarding house provided a room for us and our two dogs, temporarily. Joe teased Rick about Brooke's Point, "It's not the end of the world, but you can see it from here," then he broke out in a hearty laugh. Maybe one day the gospel would change Brooke's Point so that living in the southern part of the island wouldn't seem like the uttermost part of the earth.

A walk around the area with Joe and Fe showed us their little nipa home on a dirt road off the main road. As we continued, we passed the one bank and only gas station in town. Rick and I greeted business owners we'd known from filling purchase orders for the missionaries in the mountains. Lots of stares and a pinch or two of our children greeted us. As a courtesy, we met the mayor and informed him of our plans to start Brooke's Point Bible Church and invited him to attend. He was polite and welcoming, as is their custom.

Not much had changed, including the open market with its smells. We saw old friends and visited *Sari Sari* stores along the back roads. They reminded me of lemonade stands, except canned goods and food were sold.

Debris cluttered the shores of the sand-covered beach along the Sulu Sea. We maneuvered around it as we took in the breeze and blue waters with breaking waves. Fisherman built their nipa huts along the shore.

Joe wanted us to meet his father and we strolled together to his home. Mr. Malacao was a quiet, faithful man, a farmer, and a hard worker. Joe's mother was tiny and meek, but a strong, industrious woman.

On the walk home Rick asked, "Joe, are you ready to start the church?" We'd been in Brooke's Point one day.

"Yes. Let's begin."

Although we had no place to live yet, the four of us were eager to get started.

The next day was Wednesday. Everyone agreed a Wednesday evening prayer meeting was the perfect start to our new church.

Rick asked Joe, "Where should we hold services? We don't have a building. It would be best to meet where it promotes that this is a Philippine church, not the Americans' church."

Joe agreed, "Let's meet tomorrow for prayer meeting in my nipa hut."

Our family joined the Malacaos in their small nipa home the next evening for the first service of BPBC. We couldn't stop grinning. Our hearts filled with praise to the Lord to see the dream we believe God put in our hearts come true.

Our combined seven children gathered on the split bamboo floor and the adults sat on wooden chairs, but no one had thought about a pulpit. Rick stood up to speak but needed something to help support his Bible and notes. Pastor Joe swiftly grabbed a kitchen chair and swung it around in front of Rick. "Here, use the back of this," and we all laughed watching Rick try to balance his Bible across the back of a kitchen chair. His first sermon at BPBC on October 20, 1982, was out of Ephesians.

The following Sunday Rick brought a larger pulpit to church, the fifty-five-gallon barrel we used to ship our belongings from Manila. And the next Sunday I covered the barrel with an olive-green bed sheet, hiding a multitude of flaws. Fe and I stood back and admired our sheet-covered barrel. Every modest improvement motivated us to see what else we could do to improve the looks and meet the needs of our church.

Joe and Fe looked out for us, their American missionary partners, and helped us understand the culture and the people. This kindness made life less confusing, cut back on offenses, and proved to provide a more effective ministry among the people.

The four of us believed that biblical truths could and would transform the culture, but a transformation would require a new generation to grow up under the Bible's teachings. Scripture is alive and changes the way people think and act. We believed truth would set them free from superstitious practices and fears, which governed many of their lives.

Truth is a gift from God that we'd share with the people. The lack of God's Word created a hunger among the people to know about God and what His Word said—a missionary's dream. They knew some things but longed to know more.

To live where there was a scarcity of God's Word took an adjustment. The island remained in a backward, undeveloped state. Cleanliness, purity of life, honesty, doing things decently and in order, and if you don't work you don't eat are only a few principles we grew up with that they needed to see from His Word.

Without biblical influence to guide them, the people lived according to teachings passed down to them from their ancestors. Their teachings were followed to honor them, even after death, and to prevent being cursed by them and by evil spirits. Others developed all sorts of rituals to try to please their gods keeping generations in bondage to unnecessary practices.

Joe told us that John 3:16 had been made known to the town. He was grateful for this verse as it led to his salvation. But he wanted to learn more and teach it to his people.

When it came to evangelism, some believed as long as the tribes in the mountains looked into the sky and believed God exists, they'll go to heaven. But in John 14:6 Jesus, speaking to Thomas, said, "No man cometh unto the Father, but by me."

People everywhere needed to hear of Jesus. Even if some believed there was a God somewhere out in space, it hadn't freed them from a system of belief that delivered them from fear of evil spirits and rituals that kept them suppressed. We asked the Lord for wisdom to reach them with truth.

An Ominous House

We still needed a place to live. After a week of living in the boarding house, Fe told us the governor's home during WWII sat empty. The lower level was used for storage, but the owner said we could rent the second floor. The tall, ominous concrete house sat on the corner of Main Street and overlooked the town. No one had lived there for years. People believed it was haunted by the spirits of the dead Japanese soldiers who used the place during the war as their headquarters.

"What do you think about renting a haunted

house?" I asked Rick with a grin. "We know there are no spirits of dead Japanese soldiers inhabiting the place."

"We can't stay in this boarding room."

Neither of us was concerned about the place being haunted and were glad to finally have a place to live. Cleaning years of dirt and grime from its rooms became a challenge, but we were ready to attack it. I can still see Scott cleaning the aqua blue toilet seat. The dirt swirled around and around as he wiped the seat with a wet cloth. Toilets were rare among the homes of the people, but this one not only had a toilet but one that flushed with a bucket of water.

Rick cleaned the wide-planked dark hardwood floors, and they shined with richness. Concrete walls made the house feel unwelcoming, but paint softened the hard cement.

The faucet in the concrete sink meant I had running water. I opened the faucet and cockroach eggs came out. The water tank was full of contaminated water. Rick cut the feet out of a pair of my nylons and attached them around the faucet with a rubber band. We opened the facet to let the water drain out of the tank and watched the nylon fill with cockroach eggs.

I caught the water from the nylons in a big pot and boiled it for twenty minutes on my propane gas stove to kill the amoebas. Once the water cooled, we drank it. When we ran out of propane gas, I had a small cement grill outside on my back stairs I could fill with coconut husks used for charcoal and cook.

Our refrigerator didn't work, but it provided good storage for fresh produce bought daily at the open market. No insects or rodents could get inside to munch on our food.

Nights were so dark that Rick hired an electrician to wire the house so we could add a few lightbulbs. When the town generator worked, we'd have light. I tucked the children in their twin beds under a mosquito net for a good night's rest and then fell into my own bed.

Working the Plan

Rick and Joe went forth strategically proclaiming the gospel message daily, concentrating on the men in families. It brought joy to our hearts to lead people to the Lord Jesus. Fe and I visited homes and shared the gospel with the women. If the mother or father believed on Christ, their children came to church with them. Children didn't come on their own because some religious leaders in town told the people they'd be cursed if they came to our church.

I had trouble understanding the people when they spoke. It was disheartening to go through language school and still not be able to understand what they said. When we didn't understand what someone said, we asked our children and they always understood. The people appreciated every effort we made to speak their language. Joe told us that Brooke's Point province spoke sixteen different dialects as well as the national language of Tagalog with a Palawan accent. No wonder we had a communication gap.

We observed their way of life and asked questions to learn not only what they said but what they thought and why.

Because of families coming to know the Lord, we needed a bigger space for the church to meet. Joe found a building on Main Street that had been used to store grain that we could rent. A big sign hung on the building to advertise our church, which now was three-weeks old with four families and a few single men and ladies in attendance.

Noise from the street was a problem, but we were delighted to find a fifteen-by-twelve-foot space we could afford. Raggedy old benches without backs provided seating. They looked like they'd been eaten by termites, but none broke when we sat on them.

The two large wooden doors on the front of the church had to be left open so people could breathe. The cement walls did not allow any air to circulate and there were no windows or fans. Fe and I taught Sunday school outdoors on the sidewalk. Despite the inconveniences of the building, the church continued to grow.

Because the doors were open, a few staggered into the church who had drunk too much alcohol. Noise from motorcycles, tricycles, and *jeepneys* with no mufflers roared by the church making it hard to hear Pastor Searls's sermons. He shouted his messages with perspiration dripping from his face so people could hear the glorious gospel, "The power of God unto salvation to every one that believeth." (Romans 1:16)

Loss Turned to Gain

I embraced the laid-back ways of the Palawan people. There were times though that tried my faith. We had invaded Satan's territory and the trials proved he hated our being there.

A few weeks into our church plant, unexpected visitors showed up at Joe and Fe's home with unsettling news. Fe told me a family pulled into their front yard on a tricycle with their belongings claiming they were given permission to live there. They told Fe she had to pack their belongings and leave right away. The visitors waited in the yard for them to leave.

Joe arrived home to the scene of Fe packing their

few items as she cared for their four little boys, ages two to seven. They needed some place to go. Joe went to his father and asked if his family could stay with them until he found another place for them to live.

Once they transferred, Fe came to our place to inform us of the situation. Joe's dad had been concerned for them ever since they returned from Manila with plans to start a new church. He was in no position to keep them from being mistreated and asked them what they thought they were doing starting a church in this town? We didn't want to upset anyone, but felt compelled to do as God led.

I noticed Fe didn't seem bothered by being forced to leave her home, but rather enthusiastic as usual. She told us in her search for a place to live, she found a cement-block building with a tin roof hidden behind tall grasses at the back of town. She had already checked with the owner to see if they could rent it and he said they could. But her excitement came from the building being an ideal place for our church to meet. There was a little room in the back where her family could sleep until they found a house to rent.

Rick and I finished the boys' classes and then met Joe and Fe at the property. The area was quiet and peaceful. We wouldn't have to deal with the bothersome noise of motorcycles and tricycles. The rectangle building had a concrete floor and walls with windows on each side. The air that blew through them would be a welcomed relief after being in a stuffy building with none. Rick hoped to attach electric fans on the walls to circulate more air, as funds were provided.

Joe's family could live rent free in the tiny room behind the pulpit area until God provided something better and more private for them. Had the Lord opened a way for us to have a church building by Joe losing his home? He had.

As the four of us considered that God's blessing had come through buffeting, we thanked God for His bountiful provision, a church for the people, and a rent-free home for Joe's family. The Lord knew they had little to no money to pay rent. Nothing is too hard for Him.

It would be a lot of work to get the property cleaned and ready for services by Sunday. But when people are unified and have a mind to work, much can be accomplished—and was.

The church family got to work right away and cut the tall grasses with a hand sickle. They were happy to clear the land, plant shrubs, clean inside the building, and later paint it. The building could now be seen from the little dirt road out front.

Fe and I stood back and admired the work the men accomplished. As they built a bamboo fence, Joe stooped down on one knee to clear a section of the land for it. A man from church cut grass with his *bolo* close by him and saw the tail of a black cobra sticking out of Joe's pant leg. The man yanked the snake out of Joe's pant leg by its tail and swung his *bolo* at the snake's head, cutting it off in one swift motion.

The incident startled Joe. It took a moment for him to compose himself. When he did, he told us that the Lord used the incident to teach him that the devil sneaks error into the local church as unaware as that snake did that crawled up his pant leg. He'd need to stay alert and watch over the church to protect it from the craftiness of false teachers, the deceitfulness of sin, and the evil work of Satan, who transforms himself into an angel of light.

It blessed my heart to see both pastors walk the property together and admire the unity and hard work of the church families. Women and children were busy beautifying the grounds with plants and flowers. The building and property were being transformed just as the lives of the people had been.

Men built six new benches for seating and put backs on them. Others washed the inside of the building and prepared the cement floor for waxing. Color was added to the floor with red wax. I watched a young man buff it into the concrete with half of a coconut husk. He placed his foot on top of the rounded part of the husk and put his body's weight on it. Then he slid the flat part back and forth across the floor until the whole floor shined with a dark red tint. I tried to buff with the husk and ended up giving everyone a good laugh. The job required expertise, physical strength, and good balancing skills.

Pastor Joe's family moved into a clean place behind the pulpit area. Although all six of them had to sleep in one tiny room, they didn't mind. Fe and I stood together inside the church to take in the beauty of the finished product. I could see Fe deep in thought as she looked at the empty space beyond the six benches. With complete confidence she proclaimed, "Someday all of this empty space will be full of people."

No one was intimidated by the open space behind the six benches. It gave us room for growth. The church had grown from four adults with children to about forty people. The new building would hold one hundred and twenty adults. The men built a nipa covering on the property for the children's classes and we were ready for services.

Sunday, the church celebrated as we worshipped the Lord with praise and thanksgiving for what He had made possible. We sang hymns and studied the Word together in peaceful quietness. As people continued to come to Christ, more benches were made until the entire space filled with benches and people over time.

A man at church taught himself how to play chords on a guitar so he could play the songs we sang. Different men Rick trained stood in the pulpit to lead the singing. Everyone was satisfied as we sang from songbooks Rick purchased in Manila with hymns translated into the Tagalog language.

It was common for the church to experience *brownouts* because one generator serviced the whole town and often broke down. Kerosene lanterns and baby food jars called *kinkis* filled with kerosene gave light during services. Smoky fumes filled the air from the lantern and *kinkis*, but their light allowed us to hold ladies' and men's meetings and evening services.

Our small church building reminded me of the one little lamb a poor man owned in the Bible. The people in our church didn't possess much, but the one thing they had was their church building. They loved caring and beautifying it to show their love for the Lord Jesus. Children learned to serve the Lord by helping with church beautification and cleaning. They also served its leaders by running errands. It became popular among them to serve the Lord and His people through the church.

Several of the church family often met on the grounds to play volleyball and basketball. Children went there after school to study. Everything they did centered around the church.

There were several issues that needed to be addressed biblically, one being sanitation. Men were accustomed to relieving themselves in public. Some men thought nothing of using the side of our church building as a place to relieve themselves between services.

In a church service, Rick approached the subject delicately with Joe interpreting for clarity. He explained the need for the men to use a bathroom and reasons why.

That week the men built a *comfort room (CR)* at church. I went inside the tiny *nipa* space, or *CR*, to use it. Had I stood up my head would have gone through the thatched roof. On its dirt floor lay a two-by-six-foot board with a two-inch hole carved in its center. This would require precise aim and I'd need to squat. The men didn't have a woman in mind when they built it. I walked out. But this little space began our sanitation training.

I made an effort to assist with sanitation and taught the women the relationship between germs and illnesses. Many believed sickness came from evil spirits, and germs didn't hurt anybody. Pastor Joe and Fe helped the people understand, which helped them know Pastor Searls and I weren't teaching American culture.

Attention to Our Children

One Sunday service during the invitation, Brad went forward to publicly let the church family know he'd accepted Christ during the week and wanted to be baptized. His dad led him to the Lord after Bible class one morning. Scott also went forward, but only for baptism since he had trusted Christ before going overseas. About a year later after a Sunday service, Angie wanted to be saved but didn't understand how. At the invitation she and I stepped outside and sat on the fallen tree trunk that people gathered around after services. I explained the gospel to her and her eyes lit up.

"Mommy, now I understand. I want to be saved." She was baptized in the Sulu Sea, as Scott and Brad had been. There is nothing more precious in life than to see your children walk in truth. The Lord was good to give us our children's lives for all eternity.

Friends gave our children two more baby parrots, one from Fe for Angie's fourth birthday. Now they had four parrots and two dogs. Life was good.

Although buffetings came, blessings resulted. The love and joy in our hearts manifested itself in our church family and made me forget the difficulties—something like in childbirth.

Another surprise was around the corner; an elderly lady from our home church planned to visit us. God knew this prayer warrior would be needed for the days ahead. A spiritual storm was brewing. Satan didn't like the work we were doing for Christ and a hurricane of trials was about to hit.

Something to Ponder

The Lord often works in ways we can't understand because His thoughts are not our thoughts, and His ways aren't ours. Blessings that arise from buffeting teach us that God is in control. "For as the heavens are higher than the earth, so are my ways higher than your ways, and my thoughts than your thoughts." (Isaiah 55:9)

What blessings have come from your buffetings? What did God teach you about Himself from them? It's always important to keep looking to Jesus the author and finisher of our faith and endure hardness as a good soldier of Jesus Christ. Lean upon His strength and courage and press on. Go forward in His power and never retreat. The Christian's armor covers our front side that we can march forward in His might. Satan is the enemy, but a defeated enemy. When he tries to persuade us to believe a lie, remember that God loves us and is with us. With Christ in our vessel we can smile at the storm.

"What shall we then say to these things? If God be for us, who can be against us?" (Romans 8:31)

Prayer

Lord Jesus, thank you for watching over me and bringing the beauty of a blessing out of the darkness of a trial. You see what I need before I know what to ask, and provide it. You take care of me because you know that I'm but dust and need Your help. Your love rescues me from despair and gives me hope. Because I live in a fallen world, I experience the effects of loss, disease, and suffering. But You have told me that You have overcome the world. Help me turn to You and have rest in the presence of my enemies. Teach me how to cast all my care upon You and trust You in life. Open my eyes that I may see You in the beauty of Your holiness and not turn back from following You. Make my attitude like Simon Peter's, "Lord, to whom shall we go, thou hast the words: of eternal life." (John 6:68)

CHAPTER NINE

The Little Foxes

Rick stood on our front porch balcony overlooking the town with our visitor from the states, an elderly widow from our home church in Ohio. I'd known Mrs. Morrison since my childhood. She brought a piece of home to me and became like a godly mother to Rick. At age seventy-six, she'd never learned to drive a car, but she flew halfway across the world to be with us. She was a prayer warrior and would soon discover what a vital ministry she held in establishing our church.

I went out onto the balcony to join the two of them. Two men on the street below us began to fight. In an instant, one of them pulled out a knife and stabbed the other one. The wounded man looked up at us as he passed into eternity. The one who stabbed him ran off frightened. This wasn't the welcome we wanted for our visitor. She lowered her head and shook it back and forth in sorrow.

Our Chef

Although things about life were hard on this beautiful island, we found things to laugh about. Fe loved to cook almost as much as she loved to tell people about Jesus and she became our cook. With little money, she prepared healthy meals of fresh vegetables, fruits, and fish. Food had to be purchased every morning at the market for that day's meals. She knew how to get the best price through bartering and prepared all three meals for the day in the mornings.

Her food tasted so delicious a professional chef could have prepared it. She giggled with delight in our kitchen because she had all the ingredients she needed for recipes. Mrs. Morrison's homemade bread was a scrumptious addition to our meals. We were happy to pick all the black bugs out of the flour so she could make it.

Fe purchased a freshly caught fish at the market and sang as she prepared it for our dinner. She brought it to our table as if she was presenting a work of art and set it in front of Mrs. Morrison. We became amused at the look on her face. As she stared at the fish, its head with the eyeballs intact stared back at her. With stoic poise she stretched out her arm, and in slow motion turned the plate so the fish faced the other direction. She noticed the grins on our faces and said, "I can eat it as long as it isn't staring at me." Fe was delighted to take the head of the fish home with her and told us it's the best part of the fish. We silly Americans didn't know what part of the fish tasted the best.

Fe and I felt good about her being our cook, especially after I saw her scraping mold off a dried fish to feed to her family. Not only did we get to enjoy mouth-watering meals, but it helped provide food for their family and freed me to concentrate on school for the children.

Unusual Requests

Sometimes what the people took seriously, we found comical, like having Rick present in the operating room with the surgeon, or at the birth of their babies. It amused him as he told me one lady from church asked him to push on her belly during labor to help the baby come out. He teased her. "If I push on your stomach, the baby will fly out and hit the *swali* wall. I'll pray while you push."

I was in the middle of teaching school when Fe went into labor for their fifth child. I felt torn over the right thing to do—forgo school or forgo the birth. We'd made our children's education a priority, so we decided to divide and conquer. Rick left to be with Fe and the family, and I'd finish school, then go later. I offended Fe by not being with her through the birth of her daughter, Deborah Faith. Because we loved each other, she forgave me. It was important that neither of us held grudges for the gospel's sake. We needed each other to accomplish the task before us.

Living Among Diseases

Our family frequented Dr. Laceste's clinic due to bouts with malaria and amoebic dysentery. Common illnesses on the island included typhoid fever, dengue fever, and tuberculosis. One Sunday, a lady entered the church services who had leprosy. Rick had seen people in the mountain tribes with leprosy, but not in town. We took precautions to prevent illnesses but couldn't be one hundred percent free of the risks. We accepted the dangers knowing we were where God wanted us to be. No one caught leprosy thanks to the Lord's protection.

Malaria was as common as the flu in southern Palawan. Everyone suffered with it on occasion. Malaria mimicked a bad case of the flu—fever, headache, chills, and an aching body. Rick had it so often that he'd have to preach Sunday mornings when ill, *if possible*. God's Word wasn't weakened by his poor health. People responded to the preaching of the gospel, the power of God to salvation, and were added to the local church. This blessing kept the Malacaos and us encouraged through our many difficulties.

Pastor Joe came to the house to inform Rick a lady from church was bleeding to death. Her husband had no money to take her to the doctor. They were waiting to see what the Lord would do, take her life or spare it. Rick and Joe drove to the family's hut on the shores of the Sulu Sea, which surrounded the town.

I stayed behind to treat Angie's horrible leg sores from bug bites that became infected from playing in the dirt with her friends. Her skin was fair and dirt was her playground. I boiled guava leaves, and once they cooled, wrapped them around her legs to draw out the infection and prayed.

Rick returned from helping the family on the seashore and said they found the lady lying on the floor of their little hut with her husband beside her. They took them to the clinic for medical help because she was hemorrhaging due to a miscarriage.

"Will she be okay?" I asked.

"Yes, she's home resting now."

The lady lived to have more children and named them Rick, Carolyn, Scott, Brad, and Angelica.

I hadn't been feeling well but had no idea why. Four ladies from church knew what would cure me.

I sat on a chair while they covered me with a heavy blanket. They boiled guava leaves and put the pot of boiling water under the blanket with me.

When Rick came home from a church meeting, he considered the scene before him.

"She has *pasma* and needs to perspire to get the cold that is trapped in her body out," our friends informed him.

"How does cold get trapped in the body in the tropics?" he asked.

They explained that cold can enter the body when it gets overheated, causing the muscles to ache, the mind to be cloudy, and the body to feel sluggish—my symptoms.

"The steam from the boiled water with guava leaves will help her perspire and draw out the cold that's stuck in her body," they explained.

"I see," Rick replied as he walked away. It was just another day of our lives in Brooke's Point.

Having things explained helped me not feel so silly under the blanket. The cure seemed as strange as the illness. What could it hurt to try their treatment for an illness unique to their country?

I'm glad I followed their advice because the treatment did help. My brain didn't feel clogged anymore, and energy returned in time for me to join the team scheduled for an evangelistic meeting with a family on Saturday.

The Lady, the Farm, and Danger

Saturday came, and the Malacaos, our family, and a few others from church piled into our jeep and drove to a farm outside of town. We met the family and all their relatives, excited for this open door to share the gospel. Tables and chairs filled an area underneath a shelter for everyone to meet. The shelter was a welcomed sight as it helped protect us from the robust heat of the sun. We visited while ladies served us rice and vegetables. One lady took a special interest in serving Fe, even bowing to her.

The men began the service. As they preached the gospel, the lady kept asking Fe, "Do you care for more rice, Ma'am?"

"Yes, please." Fe felt so special.

On our way home, Fe became violently ill. She held her head out the back of the vehicle as her food came up until she had dry heaves. She believed she'd been poisoned by the lady who showed her so much kindness. Some believed poisoning Christians would earn them extra favor with their god. Two other people in our church, I was told, had also been poisoned in the past. Because it can't be proven, no one can say for certain that anyone was poisoned.

The people will tell you when smaller doses of poison were given to an individual instead of a large dose like Fe experienced, people became sick over a longer period of time. Their illness mirrored the flu or malaria. If they were treated with medication, their condition worsened. Unless they became aware of what had happened to them, they'd probably die.

I wanted to go to the police and have the woman who did this to Fe arrested, but she said it was useless because we couldn't prove she'd done it. Having to let it go was not easy, but my reason for being there was to spread God's love through Christ. He would be the Agent of change in people's lives.

Although Fe survived her ordeal, she was left with a side effect just as life threatening. She became ill a few months later and took antibiotics. Instead of getting better, she became so weak she ended up confined at Dr. Laceste's clinic. She lay on the same plywood board that Rick had his surgery on after the plane crash. She couldn't sit up or talk but was aware of what was going on around her.

Rick, Joe, and I sat by her bedside and prayed.

Dr. Laceste entered the room with more medicine. "Continue to feed her a teaspoon of this antibiotic every hour," and handed us the bottle. I put the medicine on a spoon and laid it to her mouth so she could swallow it. It didn't help her. She continued to weaken. I gasped and stood up when I saw her eyes turn glassy. Life was leaving her body. In the next minute color returned to her eyes. I relaxed, comforted she was still with us.

Fe needed better medical care, so Rick asked for help from the military to fly her to the hospital in Puerto Princesa. They agreed to do so. Joe and Rick carried her to our jeep and the four of us drove to the military's grass airfield. We were greeted by a couple military men, and they told us to lay her on a bed in the barracks and wait for the two engine Islander airplane to arrive.

While we waited, the three of us decided to pray over Fe. We laid our hands on her body and asked the Lord to spare her life. Finally, two military men informed us the airplane was ready. The Philippine airmen carried her on a stretcher to the plane and lifted her into a seat by a window.

"May I board the plane and be with my wife?" Joe pleaded.

"No, Sir. We captured a rebel and he's aboard the plane. You can't be on the plane with our prisoner."

Joe went to the window of the plane and stood on his tiptoes to reach for his wife. Although he couldn't reach that high, their sad eyes met. The longing they had to be together could be seen in their gaze towards each other. Rick had to pull Joe back from the airplane because the pilot started the engines.

We watched the plane take off and then made a beeline to pick up our children and Mrs. Morrison. All of us were deeply concerned for Fe's life. We bounced around in the jeep from the road's potholes and drove through shallow rivers where the bridges were out. We made the seven-hour trip in three-and-one-half hours.

I didn't know what to expect as we rushed into Fe's hospital room. Was she still alive? When I saw her, I couldn't believe my eyes! She was sitting up in her bed eating. She talked to us as if nothing had been wrong with her. We were thrilled, but confused. How could she recover so quickly?

"What did the doctor say was wrong with you?" we all asked.

"Tests showed I had an allergic reaction to the penicillin," then turning her head towards me our eyes met, "that you were feeding me."

I felt awful.

"You weren't allergic to penicillin before being poisoned. You've taken it lots of times. I gave you the medicine because the doctor told me to," hoping she'd understand.

She wasn't very happy with me and I couldn't blame her. I'd need to depend on the Holy Spirit's guidance going forward a whole lot more and pray about everything.

While visiting Fe, I realized my purse was missing. In all the commotion and rush to get to the hospital, it had bounced out of the doorless jeep. "Well, that purse is gone," I commented.

Mrs. Morrison looked at me with a twinkle in her eye. "Don't count on that."

On the trip back to Brooke's Point, Fe and I talked about her time at the clinic. I mentioned that I saw her eyes turn glassy. She said a dark shadowy spirit was at the bottom of her bed trying to pull her out of her body. She heard the Lord in her spirit tell it to leave her alone because it wasn't her time yet. At that moment, the dark spirit dropped her and she fell back into her body. It left.

"That must have been when I saw color come back into your eyes," I responded.

Living in this place I experienced and heard

much that was strange to me. God's Word stabilized me. He remained the same.

About halfway home from the hospital, I saw Mrs. Morrison's eyes fixed on something up ahead. "Well, look at this," she said sporting a slight grin at the Filipinos along the road.

About one hundred feet in front of us one of them held an object with a long handle that swung back and forth. What was it? — My purse!

Rick stopped beside the cheerful group so they could hand him my purse. Why were they so happy about giving me my purse? When I rewarded them for their honesty, they squealed with delight. This was so unusual that I knew the Lord had worked in their hearts in answer to Mrs. Morrison's prayers.

We continued on our way, taking our time going home. We were glad to see a bridge up ahead so we didn't have to drive through the creek. When crossing it, just as we were at its end, Rick hit the brakes. A serious drop off the bridge to the dirt road looked dangerous. But it was too late. The jeep went off the end and hit the road so hard that all of us flew into the air, smacking our heads hard on the ceiling of the *Tamara*, only to be slammed back down on our seat, hurting our backs.

I let out a shriek from the pain in my back. Others moaned. But Mrs. Morrison was injured. Her back and ribs hurt to the point she became sick to her stomach. After we got home, she rested a few more days but still didn't feel better.

Rick again battled with malaria. His constant attacks with this illness kept him in a weakened state physically. I tried not to worry about him but stay focused on our mission, as did he. The church kept growing and it amazed us. Without a doubt, the growth did not come from any special might of ours, but the Lord blessed the giving of His Word. People hungered to know what the Bible said about God.

I hoped a good night's rest would be the medicine Rick needed to recover from malaria.

Spiritual Battles

That night in our home—the haunted house— odd noises woke me in the night. I heard heavy chains being dragged across the wood floors in the sala and dining room. It sounded like someone's feet were wrapped in chains and they dragged them across the floor with each slow step they took, making the chains sound heavy to bear. I hoped no one else heard it.

Unsettled by the thought of demonic activity caused me to lie very still. Because of the malaria and mixture of medications to treat it, Rick didn't have the strength to be bothered by it.

The next morning, Mrs. Morrison told us she'd been awakened by pecking on her second-story bedroom window. She thought someone crawled up a ladder to her room. But when she looked out the window, no one was there, not even a ladder.

Hearing Mrs. Morrison's story, Scott and Brad felt comfortable enough to share their experience. "We've seen green spirits flying around in the darkness of our bedroom but didn't tell you because we didn't think you'd believe us."

We believed we were protected and safe in Christ from any demonic harm. The Spirit of God in us has power greater than he that is in the world—Satan. However, in hindsight, we could have been better prepared to live in a place where evil spirits thrived. Demonic activity wasn't this prevalent in America. Perhaps evil spirits had freer course in this remote place because people feared them and some worshipped them.

Rick's malaria didn't improve with treatment. We were on our way to Manila to see a doctor and take care of mission business. We spent the night in a hotel at Puerto Princesa before our morning flight. The jugular vein in his neck had been throbbing up and down with every beat of his heart. That evening in the hotel I watched as it intensified. He rested and wanted to read his Bible but couldn't due to the oppression he felt.

I sat by him and began to read several chapters in Psalms to him. They strengthened his spirit and comforted his soul, though his jugular vein looked like it was doing calisthenics.

That same evening Mrs. Morrison came to our room to tell us she believed it was time for her to return to the States. She'd been a blessing and we hated to see her leave but respected her decision. When in Manila we took her to the airport and saw her off, grateful she'd come.

As we watched her leave, we knew she'd pray for us and the work with greater understanding, but we didn't expect she'd send a letter to tell us she prayed for us three times a day. When she went home to heaven, we noticed a torrent of trials in our ministry, with our children, and our lives. I cried lots of tears. Her loss caused a void of intercessory prayer so needed for the ministry and the church family. This experience established deep in me the knowledge of the power of prayer and the vital role it plays.

While staying in Manila, Rick recovered easily from malaria being out of the malaria-infested area. When we returned to Brooke's Point, Rick's health stayed good for a while. I prayed often for the Lord to protect him from constant malaria attacks, but my prayers weren't being answered yet. He got sick again. It was difficult not to become discouraged.

During these times, our merciful Lord impressed upon me the purpose for Rick's poor health from Psalm 136. *Do not resent the illnesses Rick suffers. I am using all these in his life to mature him spiritually, build his character, and develop him to a place of more effective service.*

How could I resent that? I could praise my Lord, knowing He directed our steps—and stops. God's ways are not our ways. The little foxes can nibble at the vine and weaken it with each little bite, if we allow it. We have the power to resist by submitting ourselves to the Lord. The enemy ate away at our lives every way he could. But I knew God loved us. He was with us and restored Rick to a measure of health that best glorified Him. We encouraged ourselves in the Lord and rejoiced that the church was doing well.

Harder trials would soon surface. Building the church compared to taking an ax to ground covered in concrete to get to the soil. Underneath the concrete, the soil was parched and hard. It needed water, and lots of it to soften the ground to receive seed. Once the soil was ready, we could plant and wait with patience for the harvest. God would show Himself strong and teach us how to be more than conquerors in Him.

The battle is the Lord's.

Something to Ponder

Endurance in the jaws of trials is a challenge we can conquer in the power of Christ. When we're too afraid to face the unknown, and evil seems to prevail, it's easy to want to give up and get to a place where we feel safe. In those times I remind myself that the safest place I can be is where God wants me. Knowing that I'm safest in God's will and living like I believe it are two different things. In one I have a head knowledge, while in the other I possess His peace through the difficulties of life.

It takes courage that only God can give not to cower at adversity. I found prayer to be my friend and was comforted from His Word. We can go forward with great confidence in Him. Knowing we are where God wants us doing what He's led us to do, helps us mentally deal with hardships, and convinces us that all is well. The Holy Spirit in us builds our trust of the Father and strengthens our faith in Christ to enable us to live for a cause bigger than ourselves—His glory.

"Sometimes the day seems long,
Our trials hard to bear.
We're tempted to complain,
and murmur and despair
But Christ will soon appear,
to catch His Bride away.
And tears forever over, in God's eternal day.

It will be worth it all,
when we see Jesus.
Life's trials will seem so small,
when we see Christ.
One glimpse of His dear face,
all sorrows will erase.
So bravely run the race,
til we see Christ."

By Esther Kerr Rusthoi
c1941 New Spring

Prayer

Thank You for the privilege of prayer and the power it releases into our lives. You, Father, are our God. We serve You and live because of the breath of life You breathed into us. Help us remember we are at Your mercy with each breath we take and give You the honor You deserve. Thank You for life and the hope of eternal life with You one day. Until then let us go forth singing with the remembrance that any suffering here is only temporary. For we seek a greater city, one of purity and love, where sorrow does not live. Teach us to live this life with joy, for Jesus' sake, looking for the blessed hope of the appearing of our Lord Jesus Christ when my soul will cry out, "My Lord and my God." For His Namesake, Amen.

CHAPTER TEN

Tests of Faith

The sunshine filled the day with hope. New believers were being baptized in the Sulu Sea. I rejoiced in the courage they showed. Although the fear of a curse kept many away, a few became curious about what we taught and visited the church and heard the gospel. God gave the increase of souls.

One couple who had attended BPBC for six months and made a profession of faith planned to be baptized with the others this coming Sunday. But health issues persisted with the lady and made her and her husband nervous about following through with the baptism.

Before the morning service, the lady's husband came to the church to inform pastors Rick and Joe, "We were told there would be a curse on us for attending this church. My wife has been sick and we're afraid she's been cursed for being in this church. We can't go through with the baptism and won't worship here anymore."

Pastor Searls and Pastor Joe tried to explain, "God's power is greater than any curse anyone could place on you. Trust the Lord for His protection. And remember your eternal hope is in Christ."

The man was too frightened to think beyond his wife's poor health. He chose to leave the church, hoping the curse would be lifted and his wife would get better. They never returned. Life may have gotten easier for them, or it may not have. God tells us to fear Him, not what man can do to us, for He has the power to destroy both the body and the soul.

Still others trusted Christ and remained faithful, willing to face the consequences for their choice to worship with us. Whether they were ridiculed, cursed, or considered an outcast in their family, they chose to continue with us in the Lord and pray for their loved ones.

In Luke 8:4-15 we read about the seed—God's Word—and the sower—one who spreads His Word. In the parable there are four hearers given the seed of the gospel, but only one bears the fruit of spiritual life.

With the first hearer, the devil removes the seed from his heart. The second hears the good news, but when tempted, succumbs to the temptation because the seed hasn't taken root. The third seed is choked with the cares, riches, and pleasures of this life, thus spiritual life can't take root.

The Lord wants the seed of the gospel to give birth to new life in Christ that we can grow in faith. The fourth hearer did this and his life produced the works of righteousness by Jesus Christ.

How many times have I wanted to give up when trials came in like a flood? How often did the cares of this life choke me? Yet, I couldn't turn from my faith in Christ because, in answer to my prayer, He kept me faithful. He upholds His child with the right hand of His righteousness. We have nothing to boast in because all we are is thanks to Christ.

Social Behaviors

A society that has been taught Scripture takes on values established from godly principles. When the Word is not dominant, the culture takes on behavior that seems right to man but ends in destruction.

In the Word I read that I'm to set my affections on things above. If I don't know that verse is in the Bible, or what it means, I miss pleasing God and the blessing that comes as a result. It's not just my life that's affected, but all I come in contact with, and multiplies across a whole culture of people. Some of the cultural differences we faced on Palawan came as a result to what degree the people's laws and customs took form from unbiblical principles.

In general, Americans have viewed people with lots of money, prestige, and power as successful people. The Philippine people see true success by how well one gets along with others. This is so important to them that they will tell anyone what they want to hear to please them, even if it isn't the truth. This practice became a source of frustration to Rick and me.

For example, he asked his mechanic when our jeep would be fixed. The mechanic said, "Tomorrow."

He went the next day to pick it up, expecting it to be ready. But it wasn't. He asked the mechanic again when it would be ready and was told again, "Tomorrow."

This went on several days. Every time the jeep needed repaired; it was same story. From the people's point of view this wasn't telling an untruth, but pleasing us with an answer we'd like to hear. We learned not to ask. Frustration lowered as we uncovered not only the ways of the people but how they thought.

When one lives among poverty, life dictates that you find a way to survive. The Philippine people in our area lived in groups, more than as individuals. Their groups reminded me of how an insurance plan works for us. If one family is out of rice, but another family has rice, they share theirs with them. If you have meat, but other members don't, you share yours with them. If you need help building your nipa hut, the group you are part of helps you build it. This is the reason one seldom goes against their clan.

In each cluster of people there is a head. To make life work for them, everyone is expected to live according to the leader's direction. You are shamed if you go against the leader because they see you as ungrateful for the support they've given you. The saying goes— *If your nipa hut is on fire, and you need help putting it out, they'll let it burn to the ground if you don't know how to pakikisama—get along with others.*

To an American this can seem like a type of bondage because one doesn't feel the freedom of personal choice. Forms of this are prevalent in most societies, but taken to a new level where we lived. What happens if your leaders don't like your church and want you to attend theirs?

Learning how life works for the people of Palawan helped us in our evangelistic outreach. If we could reach the group leaders with the gospel and they got saved, then we had an open door to teach the Bible to the group.

Joe and Fe went against customs by starting a new church in Brooke's Point. Some considered them to be ungrateful for the teaching jobs and home they'd previously enjoyed. Being called ungrateful is one of the worst things that could be said about you. The culture dictated they pay a debt of gratitude—perhaps for a lifetime—to their influential employers. It didn't matter that Joe and Fe worked for what they had. A debt of gratitude was expected to be shown even outside of work and could bleed over into where one worshipped.

The Malacaos understood the debt of gratitude they owed was first to the Lord Jesus for their redemption. The burden Joe had to plant this church came from the Spirit of God's prompting. The Malacaos put Him above their circle of friends, their jobs, and their home. It didn't mean they weren't grateful, but if Christ was the Lord of their lives, they had to obey His leading.

Joe and Fe's decision to act independently cost them friendships and caused them ridicule and persecution. They had no home and no income, but they never complained and found ways to survive so they could serve the Lord freely.

Counting the Cost

Making choices that go against what we want, or what the culture requires, means dying to self and letting Christ reign in our hearts. I wondered how many others in town would be courageous enough to break cultural boundaries to trust Christ and make Him their Lord? God's grace enabled us to stand unmoved and He would do the same for anyone who trusted Him. Hope in my heart reigned strong because of the truth of the gospel, the protection of the Almighty, and the indwelling power of the Holy Spirit.

The Malacao children suffered often with malaria. The new doctor in town gave them a drug called Aralen, and injected it by vials into Pastor Joe's four sons. After a few years of inoculations, their skin held a yellow hue. That hue was not uncommon in Brooke's Point. The Lord filled our hearts with enough faith to trust Him to protect our children's lives.

A Lesson Learned

It's one thing to go through a hardship, but when that hardship involves your children, it tears at your very soul. It began like any other hot day in the tropical paradise of Palawan.

"Mom, can I have a goat for my birthday?" Scott asked.

I loved pleasing our children, especially on their birthdays, but a goat—really? Our house sat on cement pillars off the ground giving us plenty of yard space underneath the house for a goat. Scott was a responsible young boy of thirteen and would take care of it.

We picked up a goat for Scott at a farm, and on the way home I noticed he looked pale and acted like he didn't feel well. The scorching heat made it necessary that he drank plenty of water.

If Scott wasn't in school, he wanted to be outside working around the yard. He enjoyed planting grass seed, raking debris from the yard, and cutting grass with shears like the Filipino men did with a *sombrero* on his head.

When we got home, he joined the goat outside wearing his straw hat, and squatted down with shears to cut the patches of grass in the yard. The goat nibbled on weeds and sniffed the dirt as Scott cut. It was 2:00 in the afternoon, the hottest part of the day. He took a break for a drink of water and held onto the sink as he tried to swallow. His body weaved back and forth as he spit the water back into the cement sink. My eyes zeroed in on him.

He rushed past me to the toilet, nauseated. Once there, he fainted and went into a convulsion.

"Rick, Scott is convulsing. Help!" I screamed.

120

Rick scooped him up in his arms and we rushed to the clinic. Dr. Laceste looked at us with concern. "He's badly dehydrated and needs fluids. Carry him upstairs and I'll put him on an IV. He'll need to stay in the clinic until his symptoms go away."

Scott had a heat-stroke. How ignorant of me to allow this to happen to our son. I hadn't understood the limitations of the body in the tropical heat. Rick and I sat with Scott, while friends cared for Brad and Angie.

With Scott laying on the same plywood bed, Rick commented that he thought the fluids were beginning to bring him around.

"He's looking more alert, although the fluids are going right through him," I added.

Now I understood why the streets became bare in town in the afternoons. People stayed out of the heat and took siestas, not because they're not hard workers, but because it's necessary to survive. My mind recalled the man in Manila who asked to use our shower saying he didn't want to die. My heart went out to him. Cutting grass can be a life-threatening occupation.

The fluids flowing through Scott's veins were life-saving, but it still took three days before his symptoms cleared enough to go home. Being confined in the clinic is highly unusual. God was merciful. What a hard way to learn a lesson.

A Blessing in Disguise

Besides the diseases common in Brooke's Point, Joe also battled epileptic seizures—a possible side effect from being overdosed on Atabrine medication for malaria. Joe told us that when we started the church, he wondered what would happen to him if he had a seizure while out in the jungles preaching.

He struggled going to remote areas to witness because no medical help was available, yet he always went.

While walking to the Sulu Sea for a baptismal service after a Sunday morning service, Pastor Joe collapsed on the dirt road in a seizure. When it was over, he went home to rest and Rick did the baptisms without him. Rick preferred Joe be in the forefront with the people, so they usually baptized together.

Once we were able to visit with Joe, he told us he committed his life into the hands of the Great Physician that afternoon. He would preach the gospel in the barrios, foothills, and the mountains, and his epilepsy would not hold him back. He prayed, "Lord, if I die, I die serving You, getting the gospel to my people."

Joe never suffered another episode of epilepsy and believes God healed him.

Satan meant the seizure for evil to keep Joe from preaching the gospel, but God used the occasion to give him victory over the fear of dying in the jungles and the disease itself. Behind every opposition Satan was at work with his evil plots to convince us the work was too scary and hard to continue. But God always gave the victory.

Many of the people welcomed us into their homes to hear the good news. As is their custom, they served a *merienda* with each visit. Most knew before we arrived to offer me a coke and crackers, or bread and peanut butter, and not their cooked food. Americans have sensitive stomachs and can become ill from unfiltered water and food that's not well cleaned or strange foods we don't eat like blood sausage—meat with blood inside an animal's intestines.

On one visit, Fe called out the usual, *"Taupo,"* to let the lady know we'd arrived.

She greeted us with a giddy laugh. *"Tuloy po kayo."*—Please come in, madam, come inside.

Fe and I walked up the wooden boards into her *nipa* hut. With a big smile, she handed each of us a full plate of food. I gave a quick glance to Fe to know if I should eat it. Fe made a slight motion of no with her head as she ate the food on her plate. To prevent offending the enthusiastic lady, I moved the food around on my plate and took a few bites of the rice. That couldn't hurt. The water had to boil for the rice to cook.

As soon as the lady turned her back to get more food, Fe grabbed handfuls of my food with her hand and put it on her plate. We hadn't been given utensils and were eating with our hands. The four fingers act as a shovel to scoop up the food, then with the thumb we push it into our mouth. Before my family knew the proper way to eat with our hands, we must have looked like animals. We picked up the food with our fists and stuffed it into our mouths with food falling on us and the floor.

Fe couldn't eat all of my food and hers too. When our host turned her back, Fe took the opportunity to toss handfuls of food out the window at our backs. The self-supporting pigs would wander by and eat it. We called them this because they had to find their own food.

After the *merienda*, we explained that it was our church's goal to give the gospel to every home in southern Palawan, starting in Brooke's Point. She listened as we presented the God of the Bible to her and told her of God's gift of eternal life through Jesus Christ. We asked if she'd like to trust Christ, but with a smile she said she wanted to think about it since it was a new message to her. We thanked her for her hospitality, a value they hold in high regard.

Rick and Joe traveled daily to the outskirts of town to preach to families in the barrios. The others in the church shared Christ with their relatives and friends. Since many didn't own a Bible, they were ready to learn about who God is and the works He'd done. Those who trusted Christ joined the church and grew in their faith.

When owning a Bible is a luxury you can't afford, it can create a longing in you to know what it says. In my diary in July 1983, I wrote, "The people are eager to turn the town upside down," after hearing the good news.

One of the men in the church said he wanted to begin supporting Pastor Joe. Rick taught this scriptural principle and was pleased to see it begin to take hold. As the missionary, Rick knew he would work himself out of a job by training potential Philippine leaders in local church government.

Little Is Much with God

Fe and I decided to have fun and decorate the church with new plants. One of the men attending church came by and placed one red silk rose in a vase on the small table in front of the pulpit. Little things like this gave us abundant joy, especially when it came from the people.

With church growth, we began other ministries, such as activities for the young people. Sixty attended the first fellowship with seven making professions of faith. The ladies requested I teach a Bible class on Sunday afternoons for them. Regular early prayer meetings the first week of the month remained the secret to God's blessings of growth in my opinion.

Although the trials that tested our faith had been great, the Lord's blessings outweighed them. Much more work needed to be done to reach all of southern Palawan. The vision the pastors had needed passed on to the congregation to reach their own with the gospel in the towns, the foothills, and the mountains. More people desired Bibles and more ministries started. We had just begun.

Something to Ponder

Some comments and actions towards us along with trying events can cause confusion and put doubt in our minds. Did God really lead me? Did I do something wrong? Is God pleased? We turn to prayer and seek wisdom from God's Word to know His mind and erase doubts. The battle is won or lost in the mind. The Apostle Paul stated in Romans 7:25 "I thank God through Jesus Christ our Lord. So then with the mind I myself serve the law of God."

The Lord is faithful to bring about circumstances and encouragement just when we need it. It doesn't hurt to re-examine our steps. The Lord could show us a better way, or simply confirm to us that we're on the right path.

In all that we face, good or bad, we must stay focused, remain prayerful, and keep ourselves in the Word of God. Let us continue to move forward while "Looking unto Jesus, the author and finisher of our faith." (Hebrews 12:2)

Prayer

Thank You, Father, for giving me the grace to accept that which I cannot change and for giving me endurance so I don't faint at trials. Allow me to be strengthened through my tests of faith. Lord, You are my Protector, my Guide, and my Encourager. I'm blessed to know from John 17:9, that You pray for me. Help me not to become weary in well doing, but see what a marvelous God You are through Your deliverance. I pray that I will show my gratitude and love to You through obedience to Your Holy Word. Make my life a vessel You can use to show others Your love and draw them to Yourself. "And I [Jesus], if I be lifted up from the earth, will draw all men unto me." John 12:32 For Jesus' name sake I pray. Amen.

CHAPTER ELEVEN

Is God's Grace Enough?

Scott's life had been threatened by a sunstroke and the Malacao children's health endangered from malaria drugs. Our faith would be further tested with Brad's health crisis.

After breakfast one morning Brad developed a high fever. I laid him in our bed to keep an eye on him and checked on his fever frequently. It rose to 105 degrees. Within thirty minutes, he'd become delirious.

I yelled for Rick, "He's mumbling and rolling his head back and forth. He seemed fine when he got out of bed this morning."

Rick scooped Brad up into his arms and rushed to the *Tamara*. We couldn't get to the doctor fast enough.

We took him to the new doctor in town because she had a reputation of no one dying from malaria under her care. She examined Brad and told us he needed to be admitted to the hospital. Although not the norm, we didn't hesitate to go. We bought the medicine, IV bag, and needles for his treatment at the pharmacy in town, then drove to the hospital with Brad lying unconscious in my arms.

Tribal people lingered outside the hospital and others wandered the halls. Animals roamed freely through the corridors because there were no doors on the building or the rooms. Rick laid Brad on the bed in his room and I helped the nurse tuck the mosquito net under his vinyl covered foam mattress.

The doctor arrived to hook Brad up to the IV filled with a high dose of malaria medicine. He couldn't take oral medicine due to his unresponsive state. The doctor left but returned later that afternoon to check on his progress. She stood over him and as she examined him, stated, "He's very stubborn."

He still had a high fever and hadn't awakened or moved all day.

Rick and I squeezed into the one small, padded aqua blue chair in the room. We prayed for the Lord to bless the medicine flowing through his veins and heal our son. A tiny open window space with bars allowed sunlight into the room. They must have given us the best room in the hospital because it had a padded chair and a window.

The doctor diagnosed Brad with falciparum malaria, the kind that attacks the liver. Unless the disease is treated early, it can be fatal. We sat by his bedside as he lay motionless into the evening.

When darkness covered the sky, the black bugs came out with a vengeance and covered us like a swarm of flies. I looked at Brad and saw the mosquito net protected him from their merciless harassment.

God's grace sustained us through the lonely, dark hours of unbelievable difficulty. That night cries of people rang with heartache in the room next door. We felt the anguish of the hearts of the Palawanos in our own souls as they pounded the other side of our soiled concrete wall and wailed.

We asked the nurse what happened. She told us their young son died from malaria and pneumonia complications. Their immense loss felt no different than it would to us, or any loving parent who lost a child.

Would we lose our son? What would we do if that happened? Would we stay and finish the work?

Full of emotion we concluded that God had sent us here to accomplish a work that hadn't been completed. *If we went back home, what would we do there?*

With soul-searching sorrow, we accepted the reality that if our son passed away, going home wouldn't bring him back. We knew we belonged here for now and prayed with all of our heart that Brad would be all right. But if not, we'd finish the work God wanted us to do. With great concern for our child, all we could do was wait.

As dawn peeked its glow through the dark sky, we wished we could call our pastor in the States. We wanted to ask the church to pray for Brad, but there were no phones in town. Email and cell phones weren't on the market yet. We depended on their prayer support and asked the Holy Spirit to guide our Christian friends in their prayers for us. Feeling alone, our refuge and strength came from the God of all comfort.

Twenty-four hours passed, and Brad still lay in a coma-like state. Everyone who lived here experienced times with malaria, but this malaria left Brad lifeless. Would he ever waken?

The sun peaked over the mountains' tops in the beautiful blue sky. Rays of sunlight peered through our one little barred window. We welcomed the sight. The sun's brightness drove away the swarm of black bugs that tormented us all night and renewed our hope for Brad. The sun's rays shined through the room and onto Brad's face and motionless body.

My eyes focused on the beauty of the glowing light covering him. In the next moment I watched him open his eyes. Oh, the joy that flooded my soul.

Not only did his eyes open, but he sat up and talked to us as if the past twenty-four hours never happened. How can this be? Brad looked and talked like he'd never been ill. He didn't even feel the side effects from the malaria drugs that had gone through his system.

It sunk in that the Lord spared Brad's life. We were elated, relieved, and dumbfounded. Brad told us he felt fine and asked if he could go home.

That afternoon the doctor released him from the hospital. We drove home still mentally digesting what God had done. He'd given Brad back to us.

Having the whole family together over lunch warmed my spirits. Brad looked across the table and asked, "May I go outside to ride my bike?"

How can he be physically strong enough to go bike riding?

We quizzed him. "Are you feeling well enough to ride?"

"Yes, I'm good," with a look on his face like why shouldn't I be?

With his father's permission, he headed out the door for his bicycle. He didn't act weak from the normal effects of malaria. People have been incubated for a year after having falciparum malaria.

We watched him take off through town full of life and loads of energy. No one had loads of energy after having the flu let alone falciparum malaria. He rode back to the house puzzled by the way the people in town paused and gazed at him. "Mom, why is everyone staring at me like I'm a ghost?"

I had no idea why and gave Brad the same bewildered look he gave me. He shrugged his shoulders and walked into our bedroom. Just as he shut the bedroom door, a group of people from town walked up the steps to our front door and called "Taupo." I politely invited them inside, curious why they'd come. We'd known them since the time we lived at the flight base.

Just as the group entered the *sala*, Brad walked out of the bedroom in his carefree manner. Their eyes met. For a moment the group appeared stunned, mouths gaping as if they'd seen a ghost. Brad and I looked at them—then at each other. We didn't understand their reaction.

Soon they composed themselves as it registered that Brad stood in front of them in the flesh. They lowered their heads, a little embarrassed. One of the gentlemen explained, "We were told by the faith healer in our church that Brad died. We came to offer our condolences and sing hymns to comfort you. But I see we were mistaken. Please excuse us."

Now we knew why some people in town looked at Brad as if they'd seen a ghost. They thought he'd died and his ghost rode through town. This amused Brad. Nothing seemed to rattle him. He waved it off and went back outside to play and ride his bike. I thanked the people for their desire to be a comfort as they proceeded to leave.

God healed Brad. Now if Rick could stay well from malaria, the ministry would be so much easier. But that wasn't to be.

Powers of Darkness

Rick struggled again with another case of chronic malaria and needed medical attention for fever, chills, and headache. The new doctor said he had cerebral malaria, the kind that affects the brain. She came to our house and inserted an IV into Rick's left arm with liquid Aralen. But she didn't stop there. Along with Aralen, she prescribed Primaquine, Quinine, Atabrine, and Mefloquine orally. These drugs were potent, especially taken at the same time. After a few days of treatment, we became alarmed because the blue veins in his left arm turned bright red. We sent word for the doctor to come to the house as soon as possible.

When she arrived, she looked at his arm and began scolding him, "You are always reading your Bible. You must quit reading. You cannot get well because you won't rest your mind."

She then proceeded to remove the IV from his left arm. You can imagine how we shuddered when she immediately inserted it into a vein in his right arm. What was she thinking? The drugs were poisoning him. Shortly after she left, Rick pulled out the IV.

While he agonized with fever and chills, and took larger than normal doses of malaria medicines, he began to hallucinate. It had to be the drugs causing it. That night his whole body felt pressed and trapped under a ton of weight. He tried to pray but couldn't because of an unknown and unseen weight pinning him to the bed.

He cried out in the night, "Carolyn, I can't pray. There's such a heavy weight on me that I can't move."

I lay next to him and reached out to take his hand to pray. The moment I placed my hand in his, my hand and entire arm up to my shoulder felt the unbelievable heavy weight that was over his whole body. It felt like we were pinned under a semi-truck. With no other part of my body affected, I could pray. I asked for God's mercy and deliverance from the present hold of evil powers. This satanic attack I understood because I had experienced oppression during our missionary training over five years earlier. It prepared me for such a time as this. I knew the Lord would deliver him as He had me.

The Lord lifted the burden of weight from us as I prayed. However, the effects of the oppression left Rick physically weak. We needed Joe and Fe to come and pray with us. They were familiar with demonic opposition because this place was their home. Satan capitalized on Rick's physical weakness with malaria to attack him. Joe and Fe arrived and the four of us held hands and prayed for God to bind the forces of evil.

After Joe, Fe, and I prayed over Rick, he sat by our bedroom window to open his heart before the Lord. He wept as he saw himself before a good, loving, holy, and righteous God. The written Word brought conviction and the clarity he needed in the physical and spiritual battles he endured.

Rick looked at his right arm, veins still red. "Carolyn, I've got to see a doctor in Manila. The doctor here is killing me with these drugs."

As much as I didn't want to leave, I knew we needed to go.

That evening as I lay in bed, I reflected on my own experience with satanic oppression.

Shadows in the Night

Over five years earlier, while in mission training, I experienced a dark shadowy cloud that occasionally tormented me in the nights. It hovered above me with an overwhelming sense of the presence of evil. I'd never known this kind of darkness and it terrified me.

I asked myself, *why did this evil have the freedom to torment me?* Had I done something wrong? The unimaginable depths of evil in this dark cloud caused my entire body to shake. I'd been taken captive by something that seemed to come out of the pit of hell.

I lay in bed petrified of the haze floating towards me. It drew closer to my left side and then vanished before it got to me. Although it disappeared in an instant, it left me terrified and weak.

Would it return? The thought tormented me.

Maybe I'm losing my mind.

I definitely had a spiritual problem. But why? Shame filled me and I blamed myself. I decided not to tell anyone since the experience sounded crazy. I hoped and prayed the torment would stop. It didn't. A couple months later the same hazy cloud of malicious darkness floated towards me again.

My trembling body woke Rick and he asked, "What's wrong?"

"I'm experiencing another attack," I could barely get the words out feeling frozen from fear. Each attack left me powerless and spiritually and physically weak for a couple of days. I'm a child of God. Why couldn't I get victory over it? I needed help. But how could I explain this to anyone? Rick kept my secret for me and we prayed together for spiritual victory.

I sought the Lord's answer for deliverance from Scripture and read, "For God hath not given us the spirit of fear; but of power, and of love, and of a sound mind." (2 Timothy 1:7) and concluded the problem was me, not Satan or his demons since God had given me power, love, and a sound mind.

When yet another attack came, I decided to stop blaming myself and identify the source of my torment—Satan and his demons. I longed to exercise the sound mind the Lord had given me and became determined at that moment to get rid of my tormentor.

In the providence of God, a veteran missionary spoke to the missionary candidates in class that morning. He told us about his experience in the jungles with satanic oppression. I listened with great interest.

He and four other missionaries hiked into the jungles to reach a tribe that had never heard the gospel. That evening each of them became overpowered with an evil presence. They weren't able to overcome the evil through individual prayer.

However, when they joined together in prayer, the evil presence left, ending the oppression and enabling them to continue with their mission.

I'd found the godly person I could trust with my secret.

It took tremendous courage for me to rehearse with the veteran missionary what I'd been experiencing. Being vulnerable felt risky, but necessary. The missionary identified with my experience and knew what to do. What a relief to be understood and not judged.

The veteran missionary, mission director, and two instructors came to our little one-room apartment. They huddled around us and began to pray. I don't remember what they said, because as they prayed, a spiritual battled ensued. The demonic power didn't want to leave. But he was fighting a losing battle. "For the weapons of our warfare are not carnal, but mighty through God to the pulling down of strong holds." (2 Corinthians 10:4)

The veteran missionary didn't stop praying until my oppressor left and the battle ended. I experienced the reality of "Greater is he that is in you, than he that is in the world." (John 4:4) God's power triumphed. Going forward I maintained that victory through a disciplined thought life, that I'll share more about in a coming chapter.

I remembered the Lord impressed on me on the bus trip back to Brooke's Point when we first arrived, not to fear any of the things we'd suffer in this place for He had much people in this city. Those words brought me comfort and put peace in my heart.

I slept knowing in the morning, Rick and I would leave with the children for Manila.

Spiritual Wickedness in High Places

Scripture tells us our adversary, the devil, walks about the earth seeking whom he may devour. Satan with his army of fallen angels and demonic powers makes strategic plans to devour us. We were in territory on Palawan that Satan's army claimed. He didn't want it lost by an evangelizing missionary, or to lose souls he wanted to keep for himself.

With every church that's planted, and every soul that's saved, his cause is weakened to the glory of God. The Lord promised, "My grace is sufficient for you, for my power is made perfect in weakness." (2 Corinthians 12:9) We certainly were weak, but in His strength we stood.

"For we wrestle not against flesh and blood, but against principalities, against powers, against the rulers of the darkness of this world, against spiritual wickedness in high places." (Ephesians 6:12)

I read that principalities in that verse refer to a state ruled by a prince. We know Satan is that prince and rules a state of demonic powers. His evil powers are a supernatural evil operating in sin. He governs the rulers behind magic and demonic paganism and the demons of the air that bring evil into this world full of lies and hatred. Satan and his army possess a desire to harm people and see them suffer without a reason or cause for it. This is what is meant by "spiritual wickedness in high places" according to commentaries I've read.

The adversary possesses an organized army of demons and they run a campaign in numerous ways against God, His people, and His work. Think of military battles our country has fought. Planning went into each one. The devil is no different. He works a well-planned strategy against all God loves. He can use people to attack us, but he is behind the intended harm. We can triumph over the fierce enemy we face in the world, our sinful nature, and the devil through the believer's spiritual weapons.

The Believer's Weapons

We cannot enter into spiritual war without spiritual armor. Believers have been given six pieces of armor to overcome its powers. Verses in Ephesians 6:14-18 explain what they are and Bible notes from a Thomas Nelson study Bible for women give a description of each.

Truth acts like a belt around our waist to hold our spiritual weapons.

Obedience to truth produces the power of a godly life

The gospel of peace, our spiritual shoes, are worn to advance against the devil by taking the fight to him preaching the good news of Jesus Christ.

Faith quenches the fiery darts of the adversary by trusting Christ.

Our salvation gives us assurance and confidence in our eternal destiny.

God's Word is called the sword of the Spirit and empowers us to be more than conquerors.

Prayer causes us to stand in our armor victoriously.

Clothing ourselves in this armor prevents defeat in the spiritual battle until Jesus comes.

God Proves Faithful

The Malacaos and our family experienced a growing faith that only grew stronger in the almighty God we served. He used our trials to show His love and power, not just to us but to all who knew us.

They saw, if willing to look, that *in the crisis of life God always does right and proves faithful. (author unknown)*

We'd move forward in the work knowing "When God is for us, who can be against us?" But that doesn't keep the devil from trying because every Christian he can knock off the course of life God has for him, Satan wins a small battle. The Lord lifts us back up to fight again in the power of the Spirit to win the next one.

Sometimes Rick and I walked on the beach of the Sulu Sea to take in the sea breeze. We admired the fishermen mending their nets, preparing for the next day's fishing trip. I thought of Peter in the Bible, a fisherman and a disciple The Resurrected Lord Jesus fed Peter fish on the beach, then asked him a soul-searching question. "Simon Peter, lovest thou me?" (John 21:17)

Rick looked into the heavens and asked, "Lord, how did I get to this place?" He knew the answer. God sent him that the light of the glorious gospel could shine in the darkness and reveal Christ to the people. "Look unto me, and be ye saved, all the ends of the earth: for I am God, and there is none else." (Isaiah 45:22) The power of the gospel drew men and women to a saving knowledge of Jesus Christ.

We pondered the question Jesus asked Peter, "Lovest thou Me?" Oh, that our love for Christ would grow stronger and give us inner strength.

Something to Ponder

It takes humility to live the Christian life successfully. God is faithful to keep us needy and dependent upon Him for our own good. The cares of this life can choke us until we can't hear God's voice. He tells us in His Word that His grace is enough as we enter life's woes. "My grace is sufficient for thee:

for my strength is made perfect in weakness." (2 Corinthians 12:9)

The world, our flesh, and the devil tempt us to depend on our own understanding rather than God's grace and wisdom. Busyness can cause us to forget to look and listen to Him. How grateful we can be that in the web of circumstances He shows us the way to spiritual victory.

If we continue to tread the pathway of mercy and truth He's laid before us, we will always triumph in our Christian life. In hardships we learn He can always be trusted.

Let's make time to look to Him, learn from Him, and live a life that makes a difference eternally in His power and by His grace. For without Him we can do nothing. "I am the vine, ye are the branches: He that abideth in me, and I in him, the same bringeth forth much fruit: for without me ye can do nothing." (John 15:5)

Prayer

Lord Jesus, thank You for providing the weapons necessary to battle the spiritual war confronting me. May I be blessed to know how to use them with wisdom. Our adversary is subtle, so grant me discernment to recognize the enemy. Help me walk prepared for the battle, equipped with my spiritual armor. Thank You that You cause me to triumph over my enemies. All that comes against me You turn to my favor and Your glory.

You are my strength in times of trouble. You lift me up by Your mercy and grace that I can live above my circumstance by faith. Thank You for carrying me when I'm weak and guiding me when I don't know the way. You make rivers of water flow in the desert to give life to the weary. Let me drink from the Water of Life and be strengthened for the journey ahead. May my life be pleasing in Your sight and bring You glory, I pray for Jesus' sake. Amen.

CHAPTER TWELVE

Overcoming

Through illnesses and demonic attacks, the faith God gave me to overcome came from Hebrews 11:6: "Without faith it is impossible to please him: for he that cometh to God must believe that he is, and that he is a rewarder of them that diligently seek him."

In the verse the word *rewarder* means a continuous *deliverer*. God's deliverance wasn't just for the moment, but now and forever. I'd have no peace unless I believed it. In Ephesians 6:16 we're told faith is the weapon that quenches the fiery darts of the wicked one.

I prayed for the faith I needed to thwart Satan's fiery darts and enjoy peace of mind, not wanting to live in fear of the forces of evil. By faith I knew no matter how much adversity confronted me, the Lord Jesus would be my deliverer again, and again, and again, without end.

During the healing process of my traumatic experience battling oppression, the Lord flooded my body, soul, and spirit with His love. Perfect love casts out fear and mine was gone. I sensed that if needed, He would have sent ten thousand angels to my rescue, but all I needed was Him.

Going through the trauma of oppression, the Spirit of God opened my understanding to the importance of guarding my mind against wrong thoughts.

Just as we need to exercise our bodies, we need to exercise our minds in discipline to control what we allow in our thought life. Our minds don't need to become a parking lot to entertain thoughts that are not true, or doubts that cause worry and lead to defeated Christian living. The following verses taught me how to discipline my mind.

2 Corinthians 10:5

"Casting down imaginations, and every high thing that exalteth itself against the knowledge of God"—Don't listen to Satan's lies nor base what I believe on experiences apart from God's truth.

"Bringing into captivity every thought to the obedience of Christ"—Control what I allow my mind to ponder. Don't entertain thoughts that aren't true or allow imaginations such as thinking about the *what-ifs*.

Philippians 4:8

Whatsoever things are true, honest, just, pure, lovely, and of good report; I will think on these things—I replaced thoughts of worry and anxiety with truth and made sure my mind was full of thoughts that carried peace.

Romans 7:25

"With the mind I myself serve the law of God"—I needed to have a godly thought life in order to obey the Lord and effectively serve Him with joy.

All that I went through helped me see more of the character and power of my God. This knowledge became a vital tool in my arsenal against the deceits of Satan.

To this day I practice these truths. When I'm tempted, the Spirit brings me back to these verses and I'm rescued from the turmoil wrong thinking and worry creates.

A Pause in Plans

Rick, the children, and I arrived in Manila so Rick could get checked by a doctor there. One of his first questions was what malaria medication did he take. It shocked the doctor to hear he'd taken five malaria drugs at the same time, and one through an IV.

The doctor's response was incredible. "How are you still alive? That much medicine should have killed you."

When Rick's blood work came back, the doctor told him he didn't have malaria. Had the doctor on Palawan misdiagnosed him? Perhaps the medication healed him. We'd never know. He suffers side effects from the overdose of medication to this day.

Since Rick didn't have malaria, we wanted to get back to Palawan as soon as possible. However, we were sorely disappointed when the doctors in Manila and Palawan told us that he had to stay off the island for a period of time to allow his immune system to build back up.

He sought counsel from our pastor in Ohio using a public phone in Manila. He agreed that Rick should heed the doctors' instruction. A duplex in the Manila area would be home until we could return to Brooke's Point.

Brad and I made the trip to Palawan to gather necessary items from the house for our time in Manila. Scott stayed with his father to help care for him and Angie. Before Brad and I left, Rick wrote a letter to Pastor Joe for the church. When Joe read the letter to the people, it made them sad to hear that Pastor Searls would be gone for an extended period. Besides being concerned for him, they may have wondered what would happen to the church.

While I packed a few things, Fe informed me that

our family could transfer to a different house closer to the church. I accepted the offer, knowing this was Rick's desire as well. With the help of the men at church, we made the transfer.

Lord, Save Our Church

As if Pastor Searls being away wasn't enough to deal with, Joe told me the bank intended to foreclose on the church property we rented. It happened to be collateral on a loan the bank said the owner hadn't paid. Joe had been told we needed to vacate the property.

The people had poured their hearts into making the church what was now a clean and well cared for property. Most were poor and had so little. The church was their one little lamb. There were too many people to have church in anyone's house. We had nowhere to go. They needed the help of Pastor Searls.

Fe and I sat together and talked about the church's impossible situation. Our tears mingled together as we held onto one another and wept. The pressures of the ministry were hard to bear, so we cast our burden upon the Lord in prayer and believed we would survive all these things because this was the Lord's work.

Joe asked the men to meet him at the church every morning at 5:00 a.m. for prayer. They knelt on the hard, concrete floor and prayed every morning for one or two hours, *Lord, help us and save our church.*

We loved worshipping the Lord in this place. The men played basketball and the women watched, laughing at their mud-covered bodies on rainy days. The teens and families played volleyball on the grounds and school children went to the church after school to do their homework. Their lives were centered around the church. If we lost the property, we'd also lose Pastor Joe's home, since his family still lived in the small room behind the pulpit. Joe faced this problem in the absence of his ministry partner, Rick. We were all hurting, but not giving up.

We got all of our things transferred to the new house. I felt more comfortable and at home in this place but didn't have many days to enjoy it. With things in order, Brad and I needed to get back to Manila. Joe and Fe traveled there with us because he wanted to discuss the church issue with Rick in person. The church members remained hopeful. I told them to stay in continuous prayer for God's deliverance from losing the building.

When we arrived in Manila, Rick looked much better. Joe shared the problem about the property with him and the four of us prayed together, Rick told them he'd talk with our pastor in the states for advice. Joe and Fe visited her parents and returned to Palawan within the week.

After Rick's conversation with Pastor Dale, he said Pastor Dale wasn't surprised by the adversity. He believed the enemy moved in behind the scenes to take advantage of the situation of Rick being off the island. He understood what we were up against and became a supporting, encouraging friend. He asked Rick how much money was needed to release the church property from the loan. After telling him the amount, he asked him to call him back in three days and to spend that time in prayer.

After three days, Rick called back. The conversation exceeded our expectations. Our home church agreed to pay the amount of money owed to the bank so we could keep the church. Not only that, but the church decided to send Pastor Ron Smith, the assistant pastor, and Paul Dawson, a faithful church member, to assist Pastor Joe in the work for a couple months while Rick recovered.

Even though doctors told Rick to stay off the island, he couldn't leave the church without help in this crisis. When the money came to pay off the loan, he took it there personally. We prayed he wouldn't be robbed on the brutal road trip down the island. He carried the money in cash in a black bag to avoid delays in the payoff.

When Rick returned to Manila, he shared the details of the exciting events about the church. He headed straight to the church upon his arrival. Several of the men stayed there after prayer that morning. With great expectation, their eyes sharpened as they watched him walk towards them. Inside the church building he cracked open his black bag to reveal the cash. Their expressions of joy burst with tears of gratitude. God heard their prayers and answered.

Rick said he and Joe couldn't get to the bank fast enough. They walked in and asked to speak with the bank manager. She asked how she could help them, and they answered, "We want to pay off the loan that has the church property as collateral."

"You mean you need to know what amount of payment is due?"

"No, Ma'am, the payoff of the entire loan, please."

She accepted Rick's payment in full and gave him the deed to the property. The two men took the deed to the church, rejoicing. That Sunday morning, people's hearts were full of praise with much thanksgiving to our heavenly Father.

I remarked to Rick that adversity appeared to be the avenue God used to give us ownership of the church property. Whatever seemed against us, worked together for good. We woke up every day to a new surprise, a new blessing, and a new challenge.

When God opens a door, no man can shut it. But getting through that door takes God's faithfulness and man's willingness to trust Him through tremendous roadblocks. Each hindrance the church faced became a path to greater blessing and redounded to God's glory.

After we almost lost the church building, our home church sent money for a parsonage. Joe and Fe would always have a home for their family and a place for future pastors of BPBC. We were able to turn the little room behind the pulpit into a church office.

Seeing what the Lord did for our church made it all the harder for us to have to spend time in Manila. Our family looked forward to the day we could return. We missed Palawan and the work of establishing BPBC. Thoughts tempted me like *I surrendered to the Lord's will and look how He repaid me—with lots of grief.* But the end of the story hadn't been told yet. I would trust Him.

I had peace of mind. The young church was left in good shape. They had their Philippine pastor, Joe. Plus, Ron and Paul were coming.

Redeeming the Time

We picked up Pastor Ron and Paul at the airport and their familiar faces were a breath of fresh air. Rick and Scott left for Brooke's Point with the men to introduce them to the people, then returned to Manila right away.

I felt stripped of all incentive, energy, and motivation being in Manila away from our Palawan home and church family. But the important thing was my husband's health. We'd redeem the time where we were. We were blessed with visits from our people on Palawan when they were in Manila. God protected relationships while we were apart.

Rick had the opportunity to help a church family

meeting in a home. He preached there every Sunday morning and evening as well as Wednesday night prayer meetings. In addition to ministry, Rick took more Tagalog language classes and missionary friends gave me an opportunity to teach a weekly Bible study at a technical college, which I enjoyed.

Teaching school to our three children remained my top priority. New teaching material arrived and I needed help putting the multitude of books together for each grade, kindergarten, fourth grade, and eighth grade. Two teachers, Donna Berger Mundy and Nancy Smith from our Christian school in Ohio, came over for a couple months to help me sort it out. They were so much fun for the children and we loved having them. Manila offered the children an opportunity to take music lessons. Scott took guitar and Brad and Angie learned to play the piano. Life seemed quite normal. I wasn't used to this.

Brad approached us about buying him a portable organ so he could practice piano at home. It cost six hundred dollars, which might as well have been six thousand dollars. We didn't have the money, but we didn't tell him that. We didn't want him to grow up thinking if you served the Lord you were unable to afford an organ, or anything else. We told him to pray and ask the Lord to provide it, assuring Him that if it was what God wanted for him, He would provide it. Nothing is impossible with God.

The following month we received our support with exactly six hundred extra dollars. There had been a mix up on our support which totaled the exact amount needed. We knew this was God's answer to Brad's prayer. It felt great to tell him the good news. We went shopping for a portable organ.

News from Palawan

With little ability to communicate with our church family in Brooke's Point except through letters or telegrams, we were happy to hear from Pastor Ron that the church was doing great. But in February we received a telegram from Fe saying Pastor Joe had been admitted to Dr. Laceste's clinic with malaria and chest pains. The high doses of malaria drugs hadn't helped and his health continued to deteriorate.

Joe's illness began after a young man in our church asked him to take the gospel to his parents. They lived outside of town and were an influential couple in their community. His parents agreed to allow Pastor Joe to come and share the gospel with them.

When Pastor Joe and Fe arrived at their home, the couple's yard held large and small statues of almost every saint in their church. Inside their cement home, a tall, prominent altar came into view. Several books on magic were in their possession, and they wore amulets for protection.

After becoming acquainted, Pastor Joe opened his Bible and began to preach Christ. He showed from Scripture how their sins could be forgiven and they could have assurance of eternal life by faith in the death, burial, and resurrection of Jesus Christ, our Savior.

They had many questions and Pastor Joe let the Word of God speak for itself to answer their questions. He explained that their manmade statues couldn't protect them, help them, or answer prayers. Although the statues had mouths, eyes, ears, noses, hands, and feet, they couldn't speak, see, hear, smell, move, or walk. However, the God of the Bible is alive and can do all of those things.

In the end, his parents believed on the finished work of Jesus Christ from their hearts and trusted

Him for their protection. Joe showed them verses in the Bible that told what people did with their idols and books on magic once they were saved. They burned them.

The young man's parents decided to do the same.

People in the village saw a grand fire burning and heard what the couple burned. Many became angry. They blamed Pastor Joe for the loss of these important statues and books on magic. It created fear among the people since they believed these objects protected them. Their belief system, ingrained in them from birth, taught them that the evil spirits would have revenge on anyone who angered them. Some believed Pastor Joe would be cursed, suffer punishment, and surely die. Therefore, when Joe became severely ill and confined in Dr. Laceste's clinic, the villagers believed it resulted from angering the spirits and supposed his death was imminent.

Pastor Ron and Paul visited Joe and Fe at the clinic. Joe's chart revealed he wasn't being helped by the malaria drugs. They decided to see a doctor in Manila and notified us by telegram they were coming.

Joe and Fe traveled to Puerto Princesa to wait for a boat to Manila since they didn't have money for plane fare. Fe said the nightmare of the thirty-six-hour travel by sea with Joe already ill was miserable. They both became seasick.

Once in Manila, they went straight to a doctor's office for an examination. Joe was confined to the hospital at the University of Santo Thomas, where he underwent lab tests and a blood test called the widal test—a test for typhoid fever. He tested positive for typhoid fever. No wonder the malaria medicine didn't help him.

Besides typhoid fever, he suffered from being overdosed with malaria drugs. Now both pastors of BPBC were in Manila recuperating. Men in our

Palawan church carried on the services. They led the singing, prayed, and read Scripture and kept the church together.

Pastor Ron and Paul arrived in Manila shortly after Joe and Fe. They were ready to go back to the States. Before leaving they made sure Joe was going to be all right. The four of us thanked them for their valuable service in ministering to God's people.

With Joe in Manila, he and Rick spent time to regroup for the work of BPBC. Joe rested and in a short time recovered. The Malacaos headed home to Palawan energized for the work, and we couldn't wait to join them.

Back in Brooke's Point, people saw Pastor Joe hadn't died, but was alive, strong, and able to preach the Word.

God showed Himself strong on Joe's behalf and manifested His power as the one true living God to all willing to see it. The gospel could set people free from their fear of evil. We trusted their eyes of understanding would be opened.

The work of starting BPBC was very hard, but the water of the Word softened the parched, dry ground of hard hearts. More of the Lord's harvest was coming.

We'd be returning to Palawan soon. I couldn't wait.

Something to Ponder

When God leads us on an alternate path than we expect, it can feel like the rug is being pulled out from under us. We won't always understand why there's a bend in the road. It never occurred to me that God would remove us temporarily from the place He had called us to serve.

Location isn't as important as our relationship with Christ. He wants us to learn to trust Him as He uses circumstances to transform our lives into the image of Christ. We can get so caught up in the doing that we fail to have time alone with Him. The Lord's work becomes a burden if that happens.

We are emptied of self through the things we suffer that more of His love, patience, and kindness can be seen. His Spirit grounds us in His Word and establishes us in the faith. May we let God be God, and understand our responsibility is simply to trust and obey.

Patience. Endurance. Longsuffering. This fruit of the Spirit gives grace to redeem the time wherever God plants us. Just as the farmer who plants the crops must wait for the harvest, we sow the seed and wait on Him to give the increase. "They that wait upon the LORD shall renew [their] strength; they shall mount up with wings as eagles; they shall run, and not be weary; [and] they shall walk, and not faint." (Isaiah 40:31)

Prayer

My dear heavenly Father, help me honor You with my life. Give me words to express my love and appreciation for the gift of Your Word. The relationship I have with You is because of spending time in it. Your truth is my life and breath, bringing inner joy and peace the world doesn't know. Help me not neglect the reading of it, and grant me the wisdom I need to apply it to my life. Show me great and mighty works that You have done that I can grow in my knowledge of who You are. Help me live by the principles found in it and fill my mind with truth that I have no room to entertain doubts and fears. My dependence is upon You, Lord, to protect me from the evil lurking about that wants to take me down.

I worship in the beauty of Your holiness and await the day of Your return. One day my work on earth will be done and I'll enjoy freedom from all trials, tears, and sorrows forever. Until then I'll be grateful for the privilege of serving Jesus. In Your name I pray. Amen.

CHAPTER THIRTEEN

Making Disciples

The Lord allowed us to return to the work of BPBC after several months in Manila. We'd been there temporarily to build Rick's immune system after multiple attacks of malaria. The church family welcomed us home with open arms and prepared a *blowout* to celebrate our return. What a blessing to see the church full of people. Pastor Joe's father and mother now attended. Mr. Malacao said, "When I saw my son determined to plant this church even though the Searlses were away, I decided I needed to support him."

It felt so good to enjoy our friends, our church, and the home we'd transferred to. The morning after the party I awoke to the smell of leftover rice, fried with a little garlic, onion, and soy sauce. The familiar aroma told me I was home.

An American missionary doctor told Rick to take a small dose of a medicine called Primaquine as a prophylaxis for malaria. We all took it. We all still got malaria, but Rick never had to leave the island again because of it. Our health was also helped by installing a water filter.

BPBC had been tried and tested. God raised up both pastors from their sickbeds, strong and able to continue the ministry together.

Several farmers and fishermen attended our church. They came in T-shirts, worn-out flipflops, and shorts. We were thrilled they came no matter how they dressed. But they wanted to dress up to worship the Lord to show their love and respect to Him, so they prayed for dress clothes. The Lord provided one *barong*, one pair of dress pants, and one pair of shoes for each man. They wore them proudly and said it made them feel good about themselves.

One older farmer came to church wearing his first pair of brand-new dress shoes. He walked taking unusually high steps and mentioned to his son that the shoes didn't feel that tight in the store.

At the close of the morning message, Pastor Searls encouraged the people to confess any sin in their lives to the Lord so their fellowship with God would not be broken. The older gentleman came forward at the invitation. I watched him lift his feet extra high with each step he took.

As he walked towards the pulpit, he confessed his sins out loud with a church full of people. Rick looked at Joe for help, but he was bent over trying to hold back his laughter. Besides the man taking high steps and confessing his sins, the look on Rick's face was priceless.

Joe looked at Rick and said, "You told him to confess his sins." Now they were both trying to hold back laughter during a serious time in the service.

Afterwards, we sat with the elder farmer and discovered why his shoes were tight. They were on the wrong feet.

The church grew and with it came the need for more property. Funds were provided to purchase the lot in front of the church building and another lot behind it.

Challenged

One Sunday as people arrived for services, two men from another church were among them. They told some of the people they planned to disrupt the service by disputing Pastor Searls' and Pastor Joe's teachings. The pastors were prepared, but the visitors didn't say anything until the service ended. They challenged Rick and Joe to a public debate in the town square.

They didn't entertain the idea because of their personal conviction not to quarrel over the Scriptures—defend the faith, yes, but not argue about it. They shared the gospel with the two visitors and they left.

The church these two men belonged to had pegs anchored on the outside of their building. The members were taught that the building would go up at the rapture of the church to join Christ in the air. I suppose if you're not inside the church you get left behind according to that teaching. However, the pegs on the outside of the building allowed people to grab hold of one so they could still go up in the air to meet Christ.

Another challenge came from a different pastor who lived out of town. He visited us and said we could not preach the gospel in Brooke's Point or people would throw rocks at our house.

"We've been preaching the gospel in town for years. No one has thrown rocks at our house yet," I replied.

A day or so later, we heard rocks bouncing off our house's tin roof. We found it amusing, ignored it, and continued to reach out to people with the gospel. Opposition would always be around, so you learn to keep your eyes on the Lord and press on.

Belonging

I invited the ladies from church to our home for a time together. As we sang hymns one lady didn't want to share the songbook with me. It hurt my feelings, so after the ladies left, I asked Fe why.

She explained that our home looked so clean that she didn't want to make the songbook dirty by touching it.

"Is that the reason they don't sit on our toilet seat? I always see footprints on the seat after they use it." I asked.

"Yes," she chuckled.

I could identify, to a point, how they felt. I held similar feelings each time we went to Manila. Everything and everyone looked so much cleaner to me than we did.

After all this time, I still didn't feel accepted, but like an outsider. I'd given all I had to give of myself and felt totally spent. With nothing more to give I asked the Lord to make me the missionary He wanted me to be. I prayed they'd feel loved and fully accepted by us. In that I'd find my own acceptance.

I wanted the ladies to know I didn't think they'd make our things dirty and didn't care if they did. They were more important to me than our things. Fe talked to a few of the ladies at church and expressed how I felt about them. They were my friends. Her talk helped break the barrier between us and I began to feel accepted and a real part of the lives of the people. The Lord kept me faithful to reach out, but in His strength.

Life in Brooke's Point became fun. Our children developed relationships with the Palawan people that broke through cultural barriers. When Scott and Brad's bikes were stolen, two Filipino young men chased down the thieves and brought the boys' bikes back to them.

Scott grew a garden of Bok choy and sold it at the market. Brad helped one of our church leader's wives sell ice candy—a water-downed frozen Kool aide. It could be made if the generator worked and you had access to refrigeration.

Angie had her own set of friends and shared her dolls and bike with them.

One evening people from church came to our house to sing to us. In many ways, the Lord showed us His love and care through our church family. The actions of the people were treasured gifts.

Church growth made it possible to start additional ministries. I taught the ladies how to teach Sunday school classes and organized the materials for them. Because of the love of Christ, the relationship we shared with the church family united us. I no longer felt like a foreigner.

Every church anniversary and each New Year's Eve we celebrated with a big *blowout*, a time with lots of food, fellowship, and loads of fun. Each family donated what they could to feed the crowd.

The *blowout* wouldn't be complete without a whole piglet—the main course. They cleaned the pig and put a pole inside its mouth and pushed it through the other end. They rubbed the piglet with oil and salt, then sat by the fire all night until morning and slowly rotated the pig over an open fire to make *lechon*. A favorite part of the piglet was its fire-roasted skin.

The ladies also worked through the night preparing *pancit*, a very thin pasta with vegetables and bits of pork, along with large pots of cooked rice in abundance. A large fish called *lapu-lapu* (grouper) caught fresh that morning and pepper steak were included in the feast. Barbecued chicken on shish kebabs and fried vegetable lumpias were delicious. Tasty desserts of banana lumpia, fruit salad, and sticky rice wrapped in banana leaves satisfied my sweet tooth. Bunches of bananas decorated the tables. No silverware was needed except for serving utensils because people ate with their hands. We piled food on banana leaves until we had enough plastic plates to use.

The New Year's Eve party entertained us with an array of hilarious skits that the people wrote. Our children took part in the skits. Fe and I watched the outdoor program so amused we laughed for two straight hours until our jaws hurt. We were in pain and held our jaws to keep from laughing, but couldn't stop.

I like the verse in Psalm 37:16. "A little a righteous man hath is better than the riches of many wicked." The people didn't have material wealth, but they were rich in God's love and truth.

Training Leaders

The people in Brooke's Point lived a simple life and weren't distracted by TV, movies, or phones yet. Their favorite activity became being at church.

One month twenty-four new believers wanted to be baptized. We walked to the Sulu Sea for the service. The sea's currents were strong that day. It took the strength of both pastors to complete the baptisms.

Rick taught the church about the traditional family. Several asked questions. As best they knew how, they put into practice what they understood about the husband/wife and parent/child relationships. Obedience to God wasn't optional to them. If it was in God's Word, they submitted to it. Because Rick taught from the Bible, they treated his teachings as words from God, and not the words of man.

Rick wanted to start a men's training to prepare

the church for its future leaders. Joe was all for it and they began that Friday evening. This became a good time to pass on their vision of reaching the unreached of southern Palawan. Both pastors still believed the best way to get the good news to them was to train the church to take the gospel to their own people.

Friday training began with lots of interest and good attendance. They didn't have learning tools like concordances, dictionaries, commentaries, or the internet yet.

The men learned biblical qualifications to hold a church office from 1 Timothy. Rick concentrated his teaching in the major doctrines and taught what a local church is and its mission. The Scripture was his textbook. Sound doctrine would be the key to build a solid church foundation.

Rick shared with the men the importance of their pastor to give himself to the Word and prayer so they wouldn't expect him to do everything, although starting out it's necessary. The deacon's role would help free the pastor to give himself to this. Rick said Friday night men's classes became his favorite part of the ministry.

The women were pleased that their husbands were studying the Word and learning requirements for future leadership roles. They provided a merienda for them. Sometimes I treated the men to Joe's favorite bread, banana bread.

A few of the men in the training only had a fourth-grade education. Yet God's Spirit reigned in their hearts and He used them in His church. The men were smart but lacked education because their families were poor. Like so many, they quit school as youngsters to help in the family work.

During Sunday school one morning, Rick drew stick figures on a blackboard to represent a family. He encouraged the parents to allow all their children to finish school and emphasized the benefit to them.

The one child privileged to finish school would be expected to find a respectable job to help support all the other members of the family, including aunts, uncles, and cousins. When one works hard for what he has, but has to give it away, you can lack motivation to work.

The cycle needed broken, but that would take years. Some in the barrios didn't see the benefit of school beyond learning to read and write. They looked at it as they could eat or be educated in books. Families needed to eat to live, so education for all of their children seemed like a luxury.

Rick wanted a better life for the people. He hung a picture in the church office with an old Chinese proverb that carried an important life lesson.

Give a man a fish, he eats for a day; Teach a man to fish, he eats for a lifetime.

Although it's not a Bible verse, it could help the people learn a valuable principle for life.

When he first introduced the idea to them, the general attitude was *we are already in a pitiful condition, and Pastor Searls adds to our misery by making us work.*

Rick knew the teaching was contrary to their culture and understood how it felt when life works backwards from how you live it. He tried to encourage them and said, "I know you don't like what I'm teaching now, but one day I hope you will thank me for it. My desire is to help you know how to be responsible for your church and provide well for your families." The exception was if someone was sick and couldn't work, Rick helped them without requiring they work for the money he gave them.

If we had a church full of members because we were taking care of them, the church would not be able to stand on its own when we left. We wanted to see genuine salvation take place because of Christ's transformation in their lives.

They had difficulty grasping the principle of

Proverbs 22:7. "The rich ruleth over the poor, and the borrower is servant to the lender," because the same verse in the Tagalog Bible insinuated that the rich were to take care of the poor.

Rick said, "If you need my financial assistance, I will help you by giving you work and pay you for it. I'm trying to incorporate the biblical principle seen in 1 Thessalonians 4:11, 'Work with your own hands, as we commanded you,' and 2 Thessalonians 3:10, 'If any would not work, neither should he eat.'"

Our farmers and fishermen were hard workers. They had a tough job, but had little to show for it. They traded their goods to get what little they had.

Rick hoped that one day all the people could be independent so they didn't have to be in *utang* to others. It would give them the freedom to follow the Lord's leading in their own lives and thus in the local church. One day Rick planned to turn the church over to their leadership and they'd need to be a self-supporting, self-governing local church. We'd trust the Lord with them in what looked impossible.

Training also involved letting the people join into daily decisions for the church. When it needed a water well, the men dug a hole to find water and then put a pump over the hole. Rick searched through town for a foot valve so they wouldn't have to prime the pump each time they needed water. He got excited when he found one in town. He took it to the church for the men, but they didn't know what it was. He explained its benefit and how it worked, but they didn't want to use it. He tried again to describe how it would help them. They still didn't want it. They didn't trust it because they'd never used it.

Rick could have told them to put it on the pump anyway, but he chose not to. The goal was to get water out of the pump. If the men were more comfortable priming the pump each use, then he'd let them make the decision.

Ladies' Classes

With Rick and Joe's approval Fe and I began a ladies' fellowship with forty-five ladies in attendance the first session. With the ladies now trained as teachers for children, we started a junior church. We had them act out the Bible lessons from that morning's Sunday school lesson. This was helpful not only due to the limitation of Sunday school materials but because it got the lesson of the day into the children's minds.

They had a lot of fun marching through the wilderness with Moses, lifting a lame man over our classroom's *swali* walls, and marching around Jericho. We sang and repeated their Bible verse from Sunday school, letting volunteers quote it in junior church. It helped seal the verse to memory.

One day in my devotions, the Lord laid a verse on my heart that I could not quit thinking about. I believed it had something to do with our church but had no idea why. I shared the Scripture with Joe, Fe, and Rick. Joe knew right away what the Lord wanted. He left and came back to tell Rick that some of the couples in the church who'd been saved still lived together unmarried.

Joe approached the couples and shared Scriptures about marriage. They wanted to do right. Three couples went to the justice of the peace and asked Pastor Searls and Pastor Joe to be witnesses to their marriages. The new brides were elated and said, "Now I can say he is my husband."

Church was always rich with the Word and fellowship. One Sunday we'd been at church from 7:30 a.m. and didn't quit ministering until 1:00 a.m. In my diary I wrote, "I couldn't believe it—after being at church since 7:30 this morning, (and) a three-hour worship service, Sunday School, eats, games, and a two-hour evening service, the men from the mountains came down and wanted to have a Bible study. Both pastors were happy to teach them at the late hour.

While the men studied, the women met separately and gave testimonies of salvation until 10:15 p.m. The men were still going. The ladies were tired and wanted to go home, so we broke up our study and parted ways. When I got home, someone was waiting for Rick with questions about the Word. He came home around 11:00 p.m., happy to answer the man's questions until 12:30 a.m. While Rick talked to him, another man waited outside to talk to Rick about his Bible questions.

The hunger for God energized Rick. He met with the second man, but I had to politely excuse myself and go to bed. These were glorious times of God's Word at work in people's hearts.

The Calm of Prayer

When the church or our families needed additional prayer, Fe and I walked down the dirt street to the Sulu Sea to pray in the early hours of the morning. The sun came up over the sea as we sat on a fallen tree trunk. With the calming sounds of the ocean waves and a gentle breeze blowing on our faces, we bowed our heads and met the Lord in prayer. I cherished those moments.

Since the time we almost lost our church, the first week of the month became regular early morning opportunities to meet together in prayer. Rick and I were convinced that Brooke's Point Bible Church was not only a good church, it was going to be a great church.

A telegram from our pastor in the States was delivered to us. It said for Rick to call him as soon as possible. He'd never done that. What did he need to tell us?

Something to Ponder

Although it's hard to be set aside for a time so God can do a needed work, our time isn't wasted with Him. We can trust that He has a purpose in mind that's needful. We redeem the time by drawing closer to Him first, and then reach out to others.

Do you see any correlation between church planting and child rearing? The principle of teaching a man to fish to eat for a lifetime can be applied as we prepare our own children for life.

How can we determine if we have viewed the Bible as God's Words and not man's? Our lives can only be transformed by the Spirit as we follow its teachings.

We can identify with people of a different culture who are confronted with a change in their way of life to a degree. Once we accepted Christ, a new way of life opened up to us, especially if we trusted Christ as an adult. Our interests and desires reflect that we've become new creatures in Christ Jesus.

We carry influence in our own country by sharing Christ just as missionaries in a foreign country do. We see people who trust Christ develop values that give a culture moral integrity. Every culture needs the message of hope and truth. Let's go forth on our knees and enjoy the fruit of a joyful life as we proclaim the message of salvation to whosoever will.

How sweet are His words to us? They're a treasure money can't buy. They spare us self-inflicted troubles, protect us from evil, and cause us to grow in our knowledge of God.

165

"More to be desired *are they* than gold, yea, than much fine gold: sweeter also than honey and the honeycomb." (Psalm 19:10)

Prayer

Lord, grant me the courage to trust You as I speak of Your truth in a world that is determined to go its own way without You. Help me show others the sweetness of Your Words. May my life make a difference for Your cause. Grant me wisdom to know how to disciple others. Search my heart and show me any iniquity that would hinder answered prayer that I may confess it, be cleansed, and be a pure vessel for Your use. I'm grateful for spiritual leaders and local churches that teach truth and care for my soul. I ask in Jesus' name to live according to Your principles and commands that You will be gloried. "Thou art near, O Lord; and all thy commandments are truth." (Psalm 119:151) Amen.

CHAPTER FOURTEEN

A Change Is Coming

Religious practices in the province of Brooke's
Point were a combination of several religions
mingled together with a few traditions of their own
making. A plastic baby draped in a red cape sat on
shelves in stores and homes of many in the
lowlands. Hand-carved wooden animals sat at some
tribal doors in the mountains. Amulets were worn
by both lowlanders and mountain people to keep evil
spirits from harming them. This practice seemed
strange to us, but we hadn't grown up in a place
where fear of evil powers dominated so much of the
culture.

Parents in the lowlands pinned a square piece of
black felt to their children's clothing so no one in
passing could transfer evil spirits to them. Belts
made of rope were tied around the waists of others
to prevent being hurt by the spirits. The list goes on.

The people loved parades and had them often. A
big deal like the town festival gave them the
opportunity to celebrate with a massive procession.
A few men led the parade dressed in grass skirts
with coconut husks tied to their chests. Bracelets
made of bird feathers were tied around their wrists
and ankles. Their bodies and faces were covered in

black charcoal. These decorated men jumped gleefully in circles. They wanted the town to "Wake up. Saint Joseph is here." He was the unseen spirit over their province to bring good or bad to it. They paraded along in their special attire with cheerful spirits hoping to make him happy and laugh so his spirit would prosper the town.

Another parade was held during Holy Week. The people constructed small booths with swali walls and thatched roofs on street corners. People took turns inside the booth to pray and sing. The chanting of prayers and songs lasted until Friday at 3:00 p.m. That evening the parade started.

Hundreds, if not a thousand people paraded through town and past our house. One ten-year-old girl, named Anamie, walked barefoot on the hard dirt road as a sacrifice to God. She was dedicated and also went house to house to pray with people.

The religious leaders dressed in all black with long capes. On the cape's back a sparkly silver Z-like design flowed in the breeze. The only sound heard was their feet in flipflops walking in rhythm along the dusty road with heads down, holding a single candle to light their way.

We stood out front and watched hordes of people pass by. In the midst of the crowd, men carried platforms that held tall, life-sized mannequins. One portrayed Mary draped in blue and white. After her came a life-sized statue of Jesus nailed to the cross. Men in the demonstration bowed in respect to it, jumped in circles towards the platform and laid flower leis by the large idol of stone. More people went past us until another statue of Mary came into view draped in all black. The grim sight gave me a foreboding feeling.

Towards the end of the procession, a man-sized glass coffin with a mannequin of a dead Jesus inside sat on men's shoulders above the crowd. My heart was in my throat when I saw its neck was twisted and broken with the head raised sideways looking back. Its open eyes stared straight at me and held me captivated as the coffin passed.

While I tried to digest that scene, one of the religious leaders walked by dressed in all white with the same shiny silver Z on the back of his cape. It flapped in the wind and he turned his gaze toward us. His eyes widened with fear.

"Did you see that?" Scott exclaimed and walked inside to pace the floor. I followed him into the house.

"The man in the white cape looked at us. All these people are with him and there are only five of us, but he looked like he was afraid of us. With God, we are the majority in the crowd, just like Dad said."

I wondered what the Lord allowed the man in white to see. I remembered Paul's reaction in the Book of Acts, when he saw a town similar to this. "His spirit was stirred in him, when he saw the city wholly given to idolatry." (Acts 17:16)

On November 1, families from all over the Philippines went to their home province to be together as a family like we do at Christmas. They cooked food and took it to the graveside of their deceased parents. At the grave, they offered food to each other and ate *with* their dead loved one's spirit. Those who did this believed the spirits of their dead ancestors could see them on that one day of the year.

If the family didn't show up to express their gratitude to their deceased parent or grandparent, it could result in their ancestors withholding their blessing and leave a curse on their life. I appreciated the respect they desired to show their parents, even after death, but it seemed rooted in superstition and fear. What did the Bible have to say on the subject? That's what we would teach.

With all the fanfare of parades on special occasions, I expected Christmas to be a real *blowout.* But when Christmas came the city was quiet. It seemed odd to me they didn't have celebrations or parades that day.

Does the English Bible Teach American Culture?

In previous years before we arrived on the field, a translation from our English Bible had been translated into a Tagalog Bible. When the translators read verses that contradicted the Philippine culture, it seemed like they simply changed what it said to agree with their customs and beliefs. We discovered this during a Sunday school class Rick taught.

He took questions in Sunday school classes. From their questions he could evaluate how well they understood what he taught and if they accepted biblical truths and principles when they were contrary to their practices.

One of the faithful ladies of our church owned a Tagalog Bible. She stood up with it opened to the passage Rick taught and boldly asked, "Are you teaching us the Word of God, or are you teaching us American culture because my Bible doesn't say what your Bible says?"

What a powerful question with loads of implications. How could Rick and Joe properly teach and train the people without a reliable copy of God's Holy Word? It's man's authority on truth.

I questioned whether the translators didn't understand years ago that Americans had not changed the English Bible to suit American culture, but American culture developed from knowing scriptural principles and following them. That's something we can be thankful to our ancestors for doing.

Not only did the English Bible contradict some of their customs, but the sentence structure had been translated in the way English is spoken rather than Tagalog language structure. If our English Bible had been written in a Tagalog speaking style, much of it would make no sense to me.

Rick and Joe looked closely at the differences between the English Bible and their Tagalog Bible, especially concerning doctrine. Joe said, "Rick, I can't teach the proper meaning of grace from my Tagalog Bible. It suggests that grace is earned rather than a free gift."

The men realized the people needed a reliable copy of the Bible from the Hebrew and Greek texts. But they didn't have time to do it, nor did they have any translation training. We still tried on our own to begin one but quickly realized we needed a professional to train those gifted to do such a daunting task.

Rick and Joe decided to teach from the English Bible and have Joe translate it into Tagalog for the people. The church family hung in there with us. If the English Bible said not to partake in feasts to worship idols, and their Bible said not to judge those who took part in the feasts, as it did, the men checked to be sure truth was taught.

Teaching truth from the Word began to free the people of the bondage that held them to traditions and customs that weren't biblical. New Christians no longer worried about being cursed if they broke from their culture, when what they'd been taught had been entrenched in superstition and fear. They learned over time to trust Christ to be their protector and sufficiency.

His Unseen Hand

The Moro National Liberation Front (MNLF) fought in the mountains against the Philippine government. They wanted to separate southern Palawan from the Philippines and make it a Muslim state.

While our lives were consumed with sharing the gospel, the Philippine Marines protected the town from rebels. A rebel approached Fe and me at the market and demanded I give him my medical supplies. He wrongly assumed I had them.

Petite, daring Fe squeezed in between the rebel and me, determined to get him to leave me alone. With all three of our bodies against each other, she looked up at him, put her finger up to his face, raised her voice and declared, "She doesn't have medicine or medical supplies. They buy them at the pharmacy like all the other people in town, and she doesn't have money. Leave her alone."

He didn't believe her and shouted back. I had no idea what he said, but I saw he was as determined as Fe. In a short time, Fe managed to convince the rebel that I didn't have what he needed. It astonished me that he simply turned and walked away. Fe stood ten feet tall in my eyes. That wouldn't be the last time we'd encounter the rebels.

A visiting missionary needed to go to the airport in Puerto Princesa for his flight back to Manila. The Malacao family and ours boarded our Tamara with the missionary at 4:30 in the morning to get to the airport in time.

A short distance outside of Brooke's Point, Rick saw men with weapons standing in the road by a bridge. He knew they were the rebels because they wore tennis shoes.

When the rebels saw our green *Tamara*, they pointed their weapons at us to stop. We watched as they approached our vehicle. One walked up and pointed his M16 in Rick's face. He kept his gun on Rick while he stuck his head inside the jeep and looked around. All of us sat silent, squashed together in the back, stiff like figurines. Even the small children didn't make a sound.

The rebels talked among themselves and motioned for the man with the M16 to let us go. We learned they were planning to rob us. Perhaps one of them recognized us and knew we had no money. Whatever the case, we were set free and thankful for the Lord's protective care. When trouble came, even during times of loneliness, I pretended to take hold of God's unseen hand and wrap my hand in His. Holding onto Him, I could face life in this foreign land.

God used the attacks of the enemy to glorify Himself, promote His cause, and bless His people. The work in Brooke's Point profited spiritually, and people were being saved and added to the church despite persecution, or perhaps because of it.

Church Planting

Rick and I appreciated our pastor's counsel before we left the states. He instructed Rick to consider three areas in church planting—nature, culture, and conscience. It brought focus in the midst of such strange and confusing practices.

Nature: The missionary needs to recognize nature in the physical world around him—its plants, animals, landscape, and other features and products—and learn to live within his new environment. Missionaries aren't sent to change the environment. Our scriptural directive is to tell the people about Jesus Christ and propagate the gospel. The greatest need of mankind is to know God. As His ambassadors, our purpose is to make Him known.

That doesn't mean we don't help if there are humanitarian needs. If the people needed food, a water tank, medicine, or to be taught sanitation, as we were able, we helped, but it doesn't become our purpose.

Culture: The culture of the people is connected to their belief system. The way they think determines how they live, as it does for all cultures. What values they have and standards the people live by need to be understood. They will judge us by their standards and values, not ours. If our behaviors are offensive to their way of life, it lessens the effectiveness of our ministry.

If we understand their culture, but offend them due to an application of biblical principles, we cannot violate Scripture to please them. We explain ourselves by prayerfully contrasting their beliefs with truth, trusting the Holy Spirit to give them understanding. However, any cultural behaviors and practices that do not go against God's Word, we leave alone.

Our job isn't to make them Americans. There is a tendency to believe if people do not do things the way we do, they are wrong. The truth is that life works differently in different cultures and learning the culture can avoid many misunderstandings, offenses, and frustrations. Humility is a very important character quality among Philippine people, so we taught with the grace God gave, not thinking more highly of ourselves than we ought to.

I found it helpful after learning more of their way of life, to figure out why it developed as it did. When I could see a reason for their practices, the people's way of life made more sense. We did our best to show them how life works God's way.

Conscience: The conscience is "the part of the mind that makes you aware of your actions as being either morally right or wrong," according to the

Merriam-Webster dictionary. Everyone born into the world has been given a God-consciousness as stated in Romans 1:19: "That which may be known of God is manifest in them; for God hath showed it unto them."

The Spirit of God illuminates the person's mind that he is a sinner when we give the gospel. He needs to know he needs a Savior to forgive and cleanse him from all he's done, or will do against God. God's Spirit reveals to them that they are accepted by God by grace through faith in Jesus Christ.

As Rick practiced these three principles, it helped him make better decisions, know what ministry approaches to take, and increased his dependence upon the work of the Holy Spirit.

When we at BPBC dealt with someone who wanted to be saved, we asked questions to determine if they understood their need of a Savior and why. We'd heard of cases where people simply added Jesus to the list of gods they worshipped. They hoped the more gods they had the more it improved their chances of a good life after death. We didn't want to add more confusion to their lives, so we made sure they understood salvation comes through Jesus Christ alone.

As we continued to spread the gospel, twenty people trusted Christ in one month. For our small town, that was awesome. Others that trusted Christ joined with the twenty for our seaside baptismal service. Every trial we'd endured seemed small in comparison to the immense joy of seeing people's lives changed now and for all eternity.

Boosts of Encouragement

Having a qualified teacher for our children became more of an issue. I'd be teaching third grade, seventh grade, and eleventh grade in the new school year. The grades were far enough apart that I couldn't combine any of their classes. Kathie Collins, from our home church, joined us on the field as our children's teacher. Kathie, a gifted pianist as well as a good teacher, insisted on buying a piano in Manila. It miraculously arrived at our front door in Brooke's Point unharmed and in tune. Her music ministered to us and blessed the church as her teaching enhanced our children's education. She added to our lives in ways I didn't know our family needed. We didn't take her for granted and appreciated our home church for sending her to us.

Rick and the men concentrated on upgrades at the church. The men still had a *mind to work* and got busy building a new *nipa* classroom on the property. Its cement floor kept us out of the dirt. The women were thrilled with our new outdoor kitchen. Smoke filled the air as they cooked the food with charcoal made from coconut husks.

I taught children and ladies' classes, but I especially enjoyed teaching the teenage girls. Our first Mother-Daughter Fellowship became a special time for women.

Word arrived that Bibles International (BI) agreed to work with us on a new translation of the New Testament in Tagalog. Preparations were made for a trip to Manila for training. After the training we returned to Brooke's Point to begin the project. I contributed by typing their work into a huge computer that sat in our bedroom. We'd installed a window air conditioner to protect the computer from the heat. We benefited from that necessary addition.

In the midst of church progress and growth, wars broke out in the mountains between the MNLF and

Marines. News of it was in the headlines daily. Would the war in the mountains break out in the town?

Threats of War

We read every word in the paper to know what was happening with the MNLF.

At the start of the work in Brooke's Point, the Spirit of God had spoken from His Word individually to Joe, Rick, Fe, and my heart during our personal time of devotions. He impressed on each one of us that He was going to give us the land, but little by little. None of us asked for the land, but each of us knew it was the Lord who spoke to our hearts. It made me believe the rebels would not succeed at their mission.

A ceasefire in northern Palawan with the New People's Army (NPA), a communist group, gave us hope that the same could be true in the south with the rebels. We didn't give the fighting much thought until there would be a flare-up in town. If we took our eyes off the Lord as Peter did when he walked on water, we'd sink in the waters of doubt as Peter did. It's comforting to know that even if our faith fails, the Lord reaches out to lift us above the waters. He sets our feet on solid ground and calms the storm in our soul.

Our faith was always being tested on the island. One evening late at night, Rick heard the Marines' tank going through town. It reminded him of the sounds of war when he was in Vietnam. He jumped out of bed thinking we were being overrun by the enemy and the Marines were after them. He rushed to the front door to check out the situation. I waited with our sleeping children. Rick couldn't imagine any other reason for the tank to be going down the street than a battle ensuing.

Something to Ponder

My friends in Brooke's Point had motives that were sincere in their desire to be protected from evil and blessed by God. But sincerity didn't meet with faith. I say this because what motivated them in their actions was fear—fear of a curse, fear of not being blessed, and fear of evil spirits. What motivates us in our relationship with God?

The power of evil we witnessed in Palawan I've never seen in America making it easy to assume the powers of evil don't exist except in the minds of people. But consider what would happen in America if we lost the knowledge of the gospel? Our strong tower against the enemy would not be known. Then what?

Countries that have the privilege of religious freedom and abundant copies of the Word of God have been blessed in ways people of countries without it haven't enjoyed. May God's mercy allow us to never lose what we've been so freely given in abundance, God's precious Word. It's His truth that changes lives, families, and countries. We must resist being like the world in its way of thinking, thus its behavior and standards that are contrary to the teachings of Christ. "Be not conformed to this world, but be ye transformed by the renewing of your mind, that ye may prove what is that good and acceptable and perfect will of God." (Romans 12:2)

Prayer

Father, how can I express gratitude for the privilege of a knowledge of You and for the truth of Your Word? When I reach out for Your hand, You said in Isaiah 42:6 that You will hold my hand and keep me and make my life a light to others. Thank You for Your protection. Open my eyes anew each day to see the encouragement in front of me and be grateful. By Your grace, help me guard my heart so I'm not moved by any circumstance in life. May a merry heart develop in me from a heart of gratitude. Let me surround my mind with Scripture that my behavior, attitudes, desires, and thoughts be transformed into what is acceptable to You. You've given me confidence in place of confusion by the power of Your Word. Because the answer to this world's turmoil is Christ, He is worthy of all praise. In Jesus' name I pray. Amen.

CHAPTER FIFTEEN

Press On

Rick rushed to the front door. I could tell when he jumped out of bed at the sound of the tank, he had flashbacks from the war. We listened for any indication of trouble since he'd heard the Marines drive a tank down the street. But the town quieted, so we went back to bed. Rick explained to me that his experience with the Marines was that the tank wasn't used except in battle.

The next day he asked the Philippine Marines why they'd driven the tank through town. They said they were angry because a few teenagers had thrown rocks at their barracks. They wanted to scare them, so they went after them with their tank.

In Rick's military training, one didn't leave his base vulnerable to an attack. A Marine couldn't get sidetracked by a prank. Having a tank go down our street caused him to fear a battle ensued, especially since the paper talked of war escalating between the Marines and the MNLF.

No matter what went on around us, we had to stay focused on our mission—preach the gospel.

Every day there was much to deal with, so I had no choice but to trust the Lord to continue on in peace of mind. Angie needed to see the doctor because her lymph nodes were swollen. The doctor diagnosed her with primary complex, a condition considered a precursor to tuberculous. I'd never heard of it. He put her on a low dose of antibiotics for a year. I didn't like the diagnosis or the remedy. Was it even true? She stayed on antibiotics for months until her lymph nodes returned to normal.

No matter how careful we were with the food, even soaking lettuce in water with bleach, we all dealt with amoebic dysentery, and now Angie had it. Besides taking medication, we gave her *buko* juice, water from a young coconut, to add good bacteria to her stomach.

Our children never expressed any kind of fear, so when Angie became frightened, we paid attention. Besides her health, she heard the rumors of a possible outbreak of war in town. She felt lonesome for her friend Katie in the States and she missed her grandparents.

Her dad and I set time aside daily to spend alone with her. In the early mornings, we walked on the beach and let her talk. Making her a priority made all the difference. It didn't take long before she looked up at us with a precious smile as we strolled on the seashore and said, "I'm so happy." She was back to herself and the fear left.

Whatever situation confronted us it never stopped the work God was doing in the hearts of people. Joe, Fe, Rick, and I stood on the church grounds and watched the people enjoy each other. We felt like we witnessed a work God was doing that would otherwise have been impossible. When we say, "This work is all of Him," we mean it. We were weak, but in our weakness, His strength was manifested. "God is our refuge and strength, a very present help in trouble." (Psalm 46:1)

The church thrived and it gave us the encouragement needed to keep on going. The people broadcasted the gospel and nine more souls trusted

Christ at one Sunday morning service. In my diary I wrote, "Scott said, 'I felt the power of God in the service so strongly, I almost cried.'"

Leaders in the church began to emerge, and the translation of the New Testament showed real progress. Pastor Joe and another man in the church dropped by the house beaming with exciting news. "Pastor Searls," as they called him, "we just led a man to the Lord." They chattered nonstop giving Rick all the details.

He rejoiced with them, but inwardly felt jealous. This was the first time the men had gone out to witness without him. He knew it was foolish to be envious. After all, he'd trained and encouraged the people to reach others. The vision Rick and Joe had to reach all of southern Palawan with the message of Christ was taking hold.

When Joe and the other man left, Rick pondered the incident. He remembered when living in Manila, the Lord impressed upon him that we were to leave once he'd taught them how to establish a local church and maintain it. He sensed the time of our departure would be sooner than expected. It would take God's grace to leave when that time came.

Certain faithful men surfaced as church leaders. They followed the Lord's leading, loved God's Word, and took care of the flock. Our New Testament church plant bloomed into a functioning local church. The goals Rick and Joe set to establish an indigenous church—one that is self-supporting, self-witnessing, and self-governing—soon became a reality.

Rick needed to step aside and allow the church to operate under its Philippine leadership. It took faith to leave the church; faith that the same Holy Spirit who lives in him also lives in the people he'd taught. The Lord would direct their steps just as the Spirit of God had directed his own.

Rick and Joe discussed which men to ordain as elders, ones who could assist Pastor Joe in the oversight of the church's spiritual needs and teach the Word, and deacons to handle the finances and oversee the physical needs of the church. Joe would continue to serve as the pastor. They were in agreement about the men to ask and approached them.

Each one they asked about holding a position in the church said they could be faithful to protect the flock, felt privileged to serve, and had a desire for the office. The pastors made plans for an installation service.

Visitors from the States, Pastor Dale McCallister from our home church, Pastor Martin Masitto from a supporting church, and a good friend joined us for the special ordination service. An excited BPBC family were eager to meet Pastor Dale, the one who helped save their church and prayed for them along with others.

Pastor Masitto shared his first impression of our church. "You walk through the town and see how unclean and tired it looks. Then you come inside the church property and everything is clean and well organized."

The church was still the old, cement block building with a *nipa* hut for the children's classes, but in good shape. Paint and landscaping changed the looks of the property. Flowering shrubs, neatly trimmed grass, and the waxed cement floors inside the building made it shine. The people made the best of what we had.

What a marvelous ordination service we enjoyed. Pastor Dale preached in the morning service. God blessed with seven people trusting Christ, and several more went forward for dedication of life. Afterwards, the pastors ordained the church leaders as tears rolled down their faces.

Fe and I wept, partly because of the blessings of

the church for which we had given our all, and partly because of the dreaded goodbye. We were like family. It would be hard for them to be left on their own, yet it is what we all aimed to accomplish.

As a missionary, Rick's job was to work himself out of a job, yet as a father to a son, you never quit caring for them and helping as you are able. He comforted the people with these words. "Our departure doesn't mean we won't be available when you need us. We'll keep coming back to see you and remain involved from a distance."

The next morning, we said goodbyes and moved back to the States, since the open door for Rick was to pastor a small church there. He ended up pastoring two different churches for the next eighteen and a half years. All the while he did this, he and I made mission trips to the Philippines to encourage and strengthen the brethren and hold Bible conferences.

On one of our mission trips, I felt a moment of panic at being in Brooke's Point and wondered how in the world I'd brought our precious children to this remote island. The Spirit of God helped me see that it was by His grace. We had not only lived there but had been content in the place. I always knew His grace sustained me, but now my eyes could see the magnitude of grace He'd supplied.

I needed that same measure of grace to help me now. We still had another week in Brooke's Point. I reached out to the Lord in prayer. *Father, You've shown me how all-encompassing Your amazing grace was to me. You blinded my eyes to the backwards, disease-infested, dirty, and poverty-stricken life we lived and helped me accept my surroundings without worry or fear.*

Feeling desperate, I continued, *Lord, I need Your grace restored so I can endure another week here. I can't stand being here one more day otherwise.*

Instantly, His grace was renewed in me and I felt

good about being there. I was glad the Lord removed His grace for those few seconds so I could see how He had carried me and my family during the years we lived in Brooke's Point, a remarkable gift.

He does "exceeding abundantly above anything we could ask or think," as Ephesians 3:20 declares, "according to the power that worketh in us."

We didn't realize His plans for BPBC would go far beyond anything the Malacaos or we ever imagined, or even prayed to achieve, but God has no limits.

A Finished Project

After thirteen years the translation of the New Testament into Tagalog was complete. They called it "Ang Salita Ng *Diyos*," (ASNG), meaning The Word of God. It's not to be confused with "Ang Salita Ng *Dios*," a completely different translation.

Rick and I flew to Manila for the dedication service at First Baptist Church. We gave a copy to a special friend in Manila, Mrs. Dacanay. She told us, "I've been reading your Bible since 5:00 a.m. this morning. It is very clear, really very clear." She's a businesswoman who trusted Christ and has cared for us on our travels through Manila each year.

We were ecstatic to take our Bibles to Palawan and hold our own dedication service. Rick presented a Bible to Pastor Joe and Fe and to the lady in Sunday school who asked years ago, "Are you teaching us the Word of God, or American culture?" Her words were the spark that ignited the fire to do a new translation of the Bible.

The Sunday school children decorated a sign for Scott, Brad, and Angie with their signatures to express their appreciation to them. They held it as they sang a special number in the service. Rick presented a Bible to them on behalf of our children.

A Bible that the people could trust and understand surpassed anything we ever dreamed to come from our ministry with the help of BI.

After the dedication service, several of us went to the *nipa* place where we stayed and sat on its porch to examine the new Bible. The lady Rick gave a Bible to held it in her lap and began to read it. We watched her stop reading and look into the heavens. She clasped the Bible to her chest and hugged it with both arms. As tears ran down her cheeks, she rocked her Bible like a newborn baby proclaiming, "This is it. This is it!"

Tears welled in our eyes from hearts spilling over with gratitude that the people had a Bible they could read and understand for themselves. They could go to the Word and receive personal comfort, direction, and grace to help in time of need. What a difference that would make in their lives and the church.

Fe and I were eager to share Christ using our new Bible, so we visited a lady and let her read verses from the New Testament. She accepted Christ and we went away rejoicing that we'd led our first convert to the Lord Jesus using the ASND.

People who owned an old Tagalog Bible compared it with the new translation. They discovered many differences on their own and said they felt cheated. They hadn't known God's whole truth their entire lives.

In their old Bible, Matthew 6:33 was translated that the kingdom of God was the land around them. The ASND Bible changed it to say "the place the sovereign God rules."

Matthew 25:1 speaks of virgins in the Greek text. The previous Tagalog Bible changed the word *virgins* to *single women*. When it spoke of Mary, the mother of Jesus, translators of the ASND changed it to read an unmarried virgin. The difference was obvious to the people. They knew a single woman wasn't necessarily an unmarried virgin.

John 20:28 speaks of the deity of Christ. It was changed from "Oh my God!" in the former translation to "Oh my Lord and my God!" The former could be confused with swearing.

Acts 5:29 said, "We ought to obey God first and man." It was changed to say, "We ought to obey God rather than man."

Revelation 19:20 talks about the lake of fire. Their old translation made it a pretend place. Our translation properly changed it to a literal burning lake of fire.

The following year we made our annual Philippine trip. The change that had taken place in the lives of the people and the church was evident. Their faith had grown stronger as their knowledge of God increased. The difference was the people had a copy of God's Word and could read it for themselves.

Thanks to the support of many, the children in BPBC grew up with the ASND. They never knew anything else. As the Word of God saturated their minds and hearts, cultural practices and beliefs contrary to God's ways started to change. *There is no greater legacy a missionary can leave with the people than of a copy of God's Word. —Pastor Dale McCallister*

The people possessed a greater confidence in their evangelistic endeavors. They reached out to Dr. Laceste, who stitched Rick's face cut closed after the plane crash. It blessed us to see our people were no longer intimidated by prominent people in town and shared the gospel with them. Dr. Laceste trusted Christ and is now with the Lord. He did a fantastic job sewing Rick's face cut. Rick cared about him and was touched by his salvation.

The church wanted the truth to be known in all the land and more churches established. They prayed for their relatives in various villages to hear the gospel and have a church like theirs. I admired how fearless they were in the face of much adversity and many hardships, which included satanic oppression. They traveled into territory in the mountains and foothills where Satan was worshipped to tell them of Christ.

Outreach
Samarinana (Sah mahr en ah nah)

The village of Samarinana sat outside the town of Brooke's Point in the lowlands and could be reached by jeep. Pastor Joe preached there and several accepted Christ. He taught the people the doctrines in God's Word. Samarinana Bible Church was established using the same method of church planting as we used in the establishment of BPBC.

BPBC assisted Samarinana and provided funds to help them build a nipa church. One person stood out as the leader among the Christians and was shepherded by Pastor Joe.

Cabangaan (Cah bah ngah ahn)

Several years passed before another church plant occurred. Pastor Joe and a few of the church members went to a mountain village in Cabangaan with the gospel. Some came to know Christ as their Savior and wanted a local church in their village. Cabangaan Bible Church held their first service in February 2002. A godly man whom Pastor Joe discipled served as the church's leader.

On Rick's and my annual mission trips, we often visited Cabangaan. The Palawanos cheered when Rick said he'd visit their church. He loved going there, but the trip was hard on him because he'd become an insulin-dependent diabetic.

The only way up the mountain was to cross a river with large, sharp rocks on foot. Due to the water's strong current, the people held onto me to prevent a fall. Once across the river, we began the trek up the mountain. Sections of the climb were almost straight up. The tropical heat made it difficult to get a deep breath.

We walked in single file to keep the snakes from feeling trapped and striking us. Rick and I took a small dose of medication to lessen our chances of coming down with malaria. On one hike there, Rick became weak and unable to continue. His blood sugar dropped. A team member had a coke with her and gave it to Rick. It revived him.

After that, when the church from Cabangaan requested he visit their village, he teased and asked, "Can you provide transportation?" The tribal people promised they could. This would be something to see. Not even a motorcycle could make it up the jungle path. The Palawanos told Rick, "Even if it takes ten *carabaos* to haul you up the mountain, we will provide that for you." To gather ten *carabaos* in the mountains would be no small matter. It expressed to us how much they desired Rick's visits.

A promise made was a promise kept. When we visited them again, the Palawano men waited for us on the other side of the river with two little wooden carts and two *carabaos*. It didn't take a genius to figure out that this was our transportation. Everyone broke out in laughter.

With caution, we crossed a current of rushing water pushing against us with team members at our side. On the other side of the river, Rick and I crawled into our individual little wooden carts, which the Palawanos had put together from old lumber.

Rick twisted and turned to try to find the most

comfortable position in his cart. I sat in mine and grabbed the sides when the *carabao* took off with a jerk. A Palawano guide assigned to each *carabao* directed it up the rugged trail. Rick made sure he had a soft drink with him. He didn't want another close call with low blood sugar issues.

My body got beat up on the trek. I hurt from being banged and tossed around in the cart. The dry, hot air felt so thick I needed a breath of fresh air. I think hiking through the forest brush would have been easier than riding in that cart. Rick agreed.

When we arrived at the little church, people stood around to welcome us. The people and we giggled as we crawled out of our carts. How silly we must have looked. The church sat on top of a mountain that overlooked a beautiful scene of several forest green mountaintops. Their building was modestly constructed from bamboo. A few wood benches sat on the freshly swept dirt floor inside.

Rick told the Palawanos, "Three C's got me up the mountain, a coke, a *carabao*, and Christ."

When the service started, to say Rick and I were overjoyed to see a few of the people with a copy of the ASND would be an understatement. Palawanos who knew how to read shared what it said with others.

During the singing, some opened a large sheet of paper with words of a Ron Hamilton song. One of our men translated it with permission into the Palawano dialect—different from Tagalog. Because the people once lived in fear of evil spirits and God delivered them from the powers of darkness, their favorite song became "How can I fear, Jesus is near, He ever watches over me; Worries all cease, He gives me peace; How can I fear with Jesus?" The song testified of what God's grace had done for them.

Today Cabangaan has doubled in size and a new building was built with a nursery and classrooms for Sunday school. More churches like this were to come.

Something to Ponder

The Bible tells us if we'll follow Jesus, He will make us fishers of men. In giving out the gospel message, God doesn't hold us responsible for people's response to it, only that we give it out. The Spirit of God uses His Word to draw men to Christ.

The Lord doesn't require super saints to do His work, for there are none, or scholarly wisdom. He is our wisdom. With a heart of obedience, a life lived by faith with complete dependence upon Christ, there are no limits to what God will do through our lives. We can go forth rejoicing in the victory that is ours by faith.

Let's lift up our eyes, "and look on the fields; for they are white already to harvest." (John 4:35) The fruit God gives for laboring in His harvest field brings us great joy. "Therefore seeing we have this ministry, as we have received mercy, we faint not." (2 Corinthians 4:1) "For God, who commanded the light to shine out of darkness, hath shined in our hearts, to give the light of the knowledge of the glory of God in the face of Jesus Christ." (2 Corinthians 4:6)

Prayer

Father, help me deny myself, take up my cross and follow You. By Your grace and mercy keep me from becoming weary in well doing for in due season I'll reap if I don't faint. The trials of life can easily sidetrack me. Thank You for keeping my eyes on the prize of the high calling of Christ Jesus. When I'm hated by some and persecuted by others because of the testimony of Christ, help me not become discouraged, or quit sharing the way of salvation. Don't let me be silenced for fear of man. Thank You for those who have Your truth and receive it by faith. Your love binds us together with each other like a cord that cannot be broken. Grant me the grace to accept that whether hated or loved, my concern is that You are pleased with my life. Remind me to count my blessings, which far outweigh any suffering. By Your grace, I want to rejoice evermore, pray without ceasing, and give thanks in everything for this is the will of God in Christ Jesus concerning me. In the name of Jesus, I pray. Amen.

CHAPTER SIXTEEN

The Witch Doctor

On one of our visits to Palawan, Fe told me of Joe's ministry in the Muslim village of Sarong. His sister married a Muslim man and lived there with him in the backwoods at the foothills of the mountains. She worked as a schoolteacher in the village. This gave Joe an opportunity to ask permission to hold Bible studies in her home for the people.

Because of the custom of *pakikisama,* Joe's brother-in-law owed him a debt of gratitude because his sister taught the Muslim villagers how to read and write. He agreed to let Joe teach the Bible, but he refused to attend the studies.

Joe traveled to the area in a tricycle as far as it could take him, then hiked an additional seven miles back into the dark native village. He did this weekly for several months so the people could hear the gospel.

After one of his Bible studies, he started his walk out of the village and met Goreto, a Muslim witch doctor of the Molbog tribe, who walked the same trail. Goreto just finished leading his people in a worship of evil spirits at the *balete* tree. Joe knew the people believed the spirits lived in that tree. Part of the ceremony involved people taking food to feed the spirits as one of their sacrifices.

Joe asked, "Goreto, if the spirits have to eat the food you offered to show they accepted your sacrifice, was the food gone at the end of your ceremony?"

"No," he replied at the strange question.

"How do you know they are done eating since the food is still there?"

"As the witch doctor, I sense when they're done eating."

"If the spirits ate it, why is the food still under the tree? Who eats the food?" Joe wanted to make him think.

"The people eat the food," but he contemplated Joe's question.

"Do you have peace and joy in your life after you worship the spirits?"

"No," he responded honestly. "We know *E'mpo* as the creator God of all things and superior to Satan. However, *E'mpo* is too far away for our lives to matter to him. But Satan is close and around us every day. His power rules over our lives and mediates between *E'mpo* and us. Satan gives us good health or sickness; good fortune or bad luck, blessing or cursing, a good rice harvest or a bad one, dependent on our worship of him."

Joe opened the Scriptures and shared the gospel with him. For the first time Goreto heard God loved him and had a Son named Jesus. He knew there was a God somewhere far away in the sky, but he never knew that God provided a Savior for him.

Joe explained, "Goreto, you can have joy and peace when you worship Jesus as your Savior."

Goreto wanted peace. His gods didn't give him peace.

Joe recommended that in place of reading and memorizing Latin prayers, which he did faithfully to gain healing powers with the spirits, that Goreto read the Bible. Joe gave him one, sharing that in it he'd see how to have eternal life.

After that, Fe told us Goreto went on with his life as a witch doctor. He'd become a good best medicine man with potential of being the best around. His people admired how well he did the *tarek* dance at the celebration of the feasts to pay reverence to the spirits. It showed his gratitude for a good rice harvest. If he didn't do the dance, the evil spirits might not give them a good harvest next season.

Goreto never forgot what Joe told him and wanted to learn more about the Savior, so he read the Bible. He read about Jesus being sent by God, but he hesitated to believe in Christ because he had committed his life to Satan. He recalled Pastor Joe telling him Jesus would give him peace. He faithfully worshipped Satan, but he had no peace in his life.

As he meditated on Scripture, it broke through a powerful stronghold of Satan's, the heart of Goreto. When Joe returned to the village, Goreto approached him. "I want to accept Jesus as my Savior. I've been reading the Bible and it helped me understand God loves me and provided a Savior for me to be forgiven. I want to have peace."

Pastor Joe knelt with Goreto in prayer to the One True God. Goreto asked God's forgiveness and trusted in the finished work of Christ on the cross at Calvary. No longer did he need to fear the evil spirits all around his place because the power of God in him was greater than all the powers of evil. God delivered him from their powerful grip.

Experiencing and witnessing the reality of 1 John 4:4 never got old. Jethro (Jeth), Joe and Fe's youngest son told us when he was home from Bible college, he helped his dad spread the gospel and disciple new Christians. He went to Sarong to visit Goreto and saw that he'd not grown in his faith. Jeth talked to him about it. As he sat with Goreto on his steps, Goreto admitted it was true, he hadn't developed in his Christian faith.

"Why do you think that is?" asked Jeth.

"I have held onto my amulets. They are a family heirloom. I haven't been able to let go of them."

"Until you trust in Christ alone and give up your amulets and charms, you will not be able to grow spiritually, or experience God's peace. Your faith is either in Christ or the amulets. It cannot be in both."

Jeth shared verses of Scripture with Goreto so he could be convinced from the Word that the Spirit of God would keep him safe from the powers of the evil spirits. After reading several verses, Goreto wanted to let go of all the things he used in witchcraft, but he needed God's help to do so.

Goreto's hands shook as he passed each amulet and charm to Jeth. He handed over all his trinkets he used in healing ceremonies.

Jeth saw how he shook and how nervous he was. When he was done handing these over, Jeth asked, "Is this everything?"

"I still have the wooden case of prayers that belonged to my ancestors," he confessed. "These are the prayers I pray to be a powerful witch doctor."

With grace Jeth shared more Scripture verses to help Goreto make a complete break from his former life.

His faith strengthened with every verse Jeth shared. But when he handed over his most treasured possession, the book of prayers, his whole body shook. The two of them dug a hole in the ground and threw all the amulets, charms, and the little black book in it. They burned everything so Goreto could be free from his former life and trust Christ alone for his protection.

With all of his possessions of witchcraft gone, Goreto felt free. God was glorified in that fire. Oh, the mighty power of God's truth.

Goreto's Background

Rick and I aren't always able to visit Sarong on our mission trips because of safety issues. The Abu Sayyaf followers go there as a place to rest from their battles. It's an encouragement to Goreto and the few Christians when we can visit. On one of our mission trips, Rick and I interviewed Goreto. I wanted to learn about his life.

He was a native-born Palawano. He helped his father farm and fish, which meant he was forced to quit school after second grade. He bought the schoolbook that he had used to learn to read so he could continue to teach himself. This aided him in a significant way since he'd need to be able to read the Bible. Even before Goreto knew the Lord, God had His hand on his life.

His dad had been a Muslim witch doctor, like his father-in-law. And his uncle was known as the most powerful witch doctor on the island. Members of Goreto's tribe depended on the powers of medicine men (witch doctors) for healing and help with evil spirits.

Superstitious beliefs were a part of their way of life. When still a boy, Goreto prepared to join his father at the Sulu Sea to help fish. As he was about to leave the house, his mother cautioned. "You cannot leave yet. Don't you hear the bird singing? Certain danger is ahead. Wait for me to speak to the bird. I will ask it to watch over you."

He wouldn't consider disobeying her. That alone could bring a curse of its own. Only after his mother spoke to the bird could he go out of the house.

Growing up with a family of witchdoctors, Goreto had a strong desire to be a powerful witch doctor like his uncle. He liked the prestige and influence they had over the people. Witch doctors were better off than others financially since people paid for their services. Along with the added income from fishing and farming, he'd be able to provide a better life for his family of daily food, clothing, and shelter—as primitive as it would be.

When Goreto was a young man, he asked his uncle, "Why do you have more power than most other witch doctors?"

His uncle answered, "The key is to quote memorized Latin prayers in this little book. The more prayers I memorize and repeat throughout the day, the more healing powers I gain. If you'll memorize the prayers in the little book given you from your ancestors, and quote them every time you sit, stand, go out of the house, or go back into the house, you'll become a powerful medicine man too."

Once grown, Goreto began following his uncle's advice. He wrapped black bands around his arms and waist for protection against evil spirits and became a witch doctor. He quoted Latin prayers with almost every move he made. He had no idea what he was saying since he didn't speak Latin.

He and his fellow villagers believed evil spirits inhabited the cave on their land—a large rock that sat above ground. There were times Goreto slept in the cave to acquire greater healing powers. He led his people to lay their sacrifices at the foot of the *balete* tree where spirits lived. The gnarled tree is the largest in their village and associated with both magical and nightmarish entities. Sorcery rituals were held around it.

The villagers brought their sick to Goreto. If the person didn't get well, the witch doctor shamed the person and told them they didn't have enough faith. Or the medicine man offered to sleep, so the spirits could show him in a dream how to help the person. Often people believed they were sick because they'd been cursed or angered the spirits. Sometimes the witchcraft worked. Sometimes it didn't.

If the person's problem persisted, Goreto offered the blood of a white chicken to the spirits. He sprinkled its blood on the cave's floor as he prayed and burned incense. His ancestors taught him that the prayers rose to the spirits in the smoke of the incense.

In his prayers, he summoned the spirits to come to him with greater healing powers. If his dream showed that the spirits required a person's blood, he offered his own blood, or that of the person needing healed. He let the blood drip onto the cave's floor with the chicken's blood.

Goreto's uncle told him, "You have the potential to be a great witch doctor." This compliment made him feel elated, especially coming from his powerful uncle.

Only God can remove a stronghold such as was over Goreto's life.

He shared that he started growing in his faith after he burned all his amulets and the little black book. But his faith would be severely tested. The pressures to return to his old way of life as a witch doctor would be extreme.

Goreto's Test of Faith

Joe, Fe, Rick, and I hiked back into the humid village to have a Bible study in the little hut Goreto built with men from BPBC. The work was slow and not many in his village had trusted Christ. We were thankful to see two families and maybe twenty children, the future for the church.

Goreto shared with us how he'd suffered as a Christian in his village.

"When I found out that God in heaven loved me and gave a Savior for me, I accepted Jesus into my heart and no longer practiced witchcraft. When people came to ask me to perform healing rituals for them, I told them I no longer did that, but I'd pray

199

for them. It angered the people that I wouldn't perform magic for their healing."

The people begged, "It's important to thank the gods for the rice harvest. If you don't do the *tarek* dance to show your gratitude for the bountiful harvest, harm will come to you. Return to your old way of worship before the spirits kill you."

His wife warned him, "A curse has been placed on your life."

Goreto remained unwavering in his faith. "If the spirits kill me, they kill me. I know where I will be if I die. Do you know where you will be?"

He became ill after this and lay in his hut on his woven bamboo mat unable to speak or walk. The people, especially his family, reminded him that this was his punishment for turning his back on the spirits. Everyone believed he would die.

God gave him grace to accept his physical condition and possible death. He would not turn from his Lord and Savior, even if going back to his old way of worship would cure him.

The people reprimanded him, "See, we told you the spirits would be angry and punish you. You're going to die."

Goreto replied, "Even if I die, I cannot turn from Jesus Christ my Savior. My life is in His hands."

He lay mute on his bamboo mat, burdened for the souls of his people. How he longed to see them trust the Lord Jesus and be delivered from the oppression of evil. They too could have peace and be assured of a home in heaven with God.

To the people's amazement, instead of Goreto losing his life, the Lord raised him up off his sickbed. His people beheld the power of the living and true God through this. God tested Goreto's faith and used his life to reveal Himself stronger than the spirits the people worshipped. Once again, we see the reality of I John 4:4 in action.

They asked, "How is it you are still alive?" and he told them about Jesus. The teachings of Christ were strange to the ears of the people. It frightened them to have teachings that taught them to turn from worshipping evil spirits.

After this Goreto chopped down the *balete* tree where he once worshipped evil spirits, and used the wood for posts to build a little *nipa* church on land close to his hut. Pastor Joe and he named it Sarong Bible Church. BPBC sent a man there to teach God's truth.

Now young people in the church pass out tracts in the village and witness to their parents. The parents gave permission for them to attend BPBC youth camps each year. Goreto thanks them with a small token of appreciation. Several have been saved as a result of the camps.

Goreto rejoices over the children accepting Christ too. His heart's desire is for the young people to learn to read. Then they can read the Bible and continue to spread the gospel among the villagers for generations to come.

Goreto wept as he told us about all the years he'd prayed for his siblings. Not one had trusted Christ. They relentlessly pressured him to return to his old ways. He cried as he said, "The Lord has not given me even one sibling."

I knew how good he was at memorizing and suggested, "The next time your siblings come to you to get you to turn back to your former ways of worship, be prepared with memorized salvation verses." I gave him a list to memorize. "When they begin begging you to return to the worship of evil spirits and dance the *tarek* dance, begin quoting Bible verses." He did this and the Lord saved one of his siblings after eleven years of praying. He has hope more will trust Christ.

In 2016, a group of Muslims came to his village from another island in hopes they could elect their Muslim candidate for mayor of Brooke's Point. They threatened Goreto's life. He assumed he was going to be killed. He spoke with the young man from BPBC who preached in the church services at Sarong. "If I am killed, be sure you carry on the work here." Goreto told me his life didn't matter to him but preaching the gospel to his people did. God spared his life and he continues to tell his people about Jesus. The church continues to grow little by little. Goreto's face glows with inner joy and peace that God has given him. It is priceless.

Time to start another church.

Something to Ponder

Is there a greater manifestation of the love of God in His creation than His gift of a transformed life? God has made us new creatures in Christ Jesus and joined us to His glorious life. "Therefore, if any man be in Christ, he is a new creature: old things are passed away; behold, all things are become new." (2 Corinthians 5:17)

How did Goreto have the courage to face possible death without turning back to his old ways? How does any Christian face possible death for their faith? It's by abiding in Him. We receive Him by faith and we live each day by faith.

Goreto had promised his life to Satan. Yet, even that did not keep the Lord from showing the witch doctor His mercy and grace. "For whosoever shall call upon the name of the Lord shall be saved." (Romans 10:13) God has His hand on our lives before we even know Him.

In the Bible we're told witchcraft is a work of the flesh and it was a temptation to Goreto. We also face temptations. We can trust Christ to give grace to overcome them as Goreto had to do. With each victory we grow more established in our faith. God has given us His divine nature so we can be victorious. (2 Peter 1:4)

Prayer

Lord Jesus, I thank You for making me a new creature in Christ. Old things are passed away and all things have become new. Where I lack spiritual growth, I invite You into my life to teach me more of You that I may grow thereby. I want to do what I should but often fall short of being the person You desire. Help me not take advantage of Your mercy and grace but give You the honor, respect, and love You deserve. I ask Your help to keep me abiding in Christ, through all of life.

I will trust You to accomplish Your purpose for Your glory through each trial and each blessing. I've seen Your grace at work in people's lives and how You've made something beautiful from ruins. Make my life a trophy of Your grace and let it be the rejoicing of Your heart. I pray in Jesus' name. Amen.

CHAPTER SEVENTEEN

Claiming Territory for Christ

With a strong, established church, a growing number of young men and women were ready to spread the gospel to more villages. Members of BPBC continued to reach out to family in other areas of the island. Children who had grown up in the church were now able to help Pastor Joe, including his own children. With boldness, they proclaimed the death, burial, and resurrection of Christ wherever they went.

Puerto Princesa

Joe and Fe's only daughter, Deborah, became a professor in mass communications in Puerto Princesa for the University of Palawan. Several young people from Brooke's Point, among others on the island, took her classes.

In the Philippines, the government sees it as a good thing to speak of God and study the Bible. You can witness in schools, colleges, and businesses with no problem. Deborah ministered to several of her students in prayer and the Word and led more than a few of them to Christ.

The students from Brooke's Point missed BPBC and prayed for a church like it in Puerto Princesa. Deborah asked her father to pray about starting a church there. He and the church members prayed for God's will and the church began. At first the group met in a room at the university. Puerto Princesa Bible Church continues to this day. The church now meets in another building. They have met their own trials with faith.

Matiyaga (Mah tee yah gah)

Rick and I celebrated the twenty-fifth anniversary of BPBC on the island with the people. While there, Pastor Joe took us to Matiyaga to meet Calyon. He was a native Palawano and the leader of his village in the remote foothills.

Rick taught the Word to the people and afterwards, Calyon asked to speak with Rick and Joe. He explained, "I practiced ancestor and animistic worship as a young man along with my people. But when I looked into the heavens, I believed there had to be a God who created everything. My people and I believed we'd live after we died in the spirit world, but I longed to know more about how to have life with God.

"In my search for answers, a villager said, 'Do you see that mountain? If you'll make your way through the dense brush to its highest peak, you'll find eternal life.' I hiked alone up the rocky hills, barefoot, until I reached the top of the mountain. Once there, I looked all around and into the skies trying to find life that lasted forever. While I searched, a storm came up and a bolt of lightning struck the mountain. It split the ground where I stood and scared me. My people believe lightning carries a curse in it. Horrified, I got off the mountain as soon as possible. I felt disappointed that I didn't find my answer to life after death as I made my way home.

"On the way back to my village, I met a man hiking up the trail. I asked if he knew where I could find eternal life. But before he could answer me, a small airplane flew over us. Pointing to the plane, the man told me the person who flies the dragonfly had a black book. In it he would show me how to have life eternal—*if* I could find him."

Rick interrupted Calyon to ask if he knew when the plane had flown over him. He gave the year, and it was the same time Rick piloted the plane. It could've been Rick who flew over them that day.

Calyon continued. "It took years to find someone who could tell me about Jesus, God's Son, and explain how I could be accepted into heaven. I don't want my children, or the people in my village, to go through what I went through. With a church, they can be taught the Word of God for generations to come. Will you help my people have a church where truth is taught?"

His request tore at Rick's and Joe's hearts. They prayed for someone to send to Matiyaga from BPBC to teach the Word to Calyon and his people. A few men started going there once a week. Several trusted Christ and Matiyaga Bible Church began. Today Calyon is with the Lord. He left this world with a church for his people who can read their own copy of the Word of God. Today a new church building with a concrete foundation has been erected.

Tabud (Tah bood)

Even our outreach churches were witnessing and one mission outreach began from Samarinana Bible Church called Tabud Bible Missions. A team from their church with our help assisted the brethren. The son of Pastor Joe, Jeriel (Jay) was assigned as its weekly Bible teacher until it had its own pastor and church leaders.

Tabud's church family meets in a simple building with a dirt floor, grass roof, and swali walls. A storm with high winds destroyed their first building. Supporting churches from the States provided new nipa materials and the people rebuilt. Then they lost their land and were forced to move their church materials to a different location. The people didn't give up but kept the small church going and made humble improvements in their little building. It reminded me of the one red rose that a man brought to BPBC church many years earlier during our humble beginnings. Pastor Joe and Fe often encourage the poor churches in the outreaches by letting them know we began BPBC in a nipa home. Little is much when God is in it.

Today a new church building with a concrete foundation has been erected.

Tatandayan (Tah tahn dah yahn)

Another hour's hike from Cabangaan was a mountain church at Tatandayan. The church was started years earlier by a former mission group. Their church leaders visited us to ask for help in teaching the Word. What they knew about the Scriptures agreed with our teachings, but they wanted to learn more about the Bible. They too wanted to reach the mountain tribes who didn't have a gospel witness.

Those who helped start their church were no longer in southern Palawan. The people chose to become a part of Southern Palawan Ministries but remained an independent New Testament church, which is the goal for all our church plants. The Tatandayan church would be a strategic partner in our evangelistic efforts in the mountains, and we were an important component in training them and teaching biblical principles to reach our common *goal.*

Tagpinasao and Bilang Bilang Bible Missions (Tahg pee nah sahowl and Bee lahng Bee lahng)

A church member at BPBC had a family member who lived in the area of Tagpinasao. They offered their place to us for Bible studies. Tagpinasao and Bilang Bilang were close to each other, so our evangelistic team combined Bible classes for the two villages. The Bible teacher taught from the beginning of man in Genesis to the crucifixion and resurrection of Jesus Christ.

The outreach grew and became known as Tagpinasao and Bilang Bilang Bible Missions. Men from that area have been trained in the Word to hold the Bible studies. It's not yet a church, but the workers are seeing people saved. When they grow in their faith and decide they want a church, we will be there to assist them.

Barong Barong Bible Missions (Bah wrung Bah Wrung)

Barong Barong Bible Missions began through a ministry of Jay and another man at Samarinana. The mayor of Brooke's Point asked Jay to be the project manager to build one of the hanging bridges over the rivers in the foothills. Mayor Jean wanted to better the peoples' lives with the hanging bridges. The Palawanos in the mountains wouldn't have to wade through the rivers or wait for low tide to go to market. On one of our hikes back to town from visiting Matiyaga, Jeth almost drowned trying to push the motorcycle across a strong current of water.

Jay witnessed to the man who supplied the lumber for the bridge he worked on, and led him to the Lord. The man was from the village of Barong Barong. There was a family attending Samarinana Bible Church who also lived in Barong Barong. Jay visited the place and saw it was full of children, eager to hear Bible stories. Thus, Jay preached in the village and organized the believers into a regular Bible study.

Tubtub (Tube tube)

Rick and I happened to be on the island when a box of clothing arrived from our church in Taylors, South Carolina. We delivered them to an outreach in Tubtub. The people were eager to be taught the Bible. I looked around the grounds and saw adults sitting inside a nipa hut, a group of teens under a tree, while young children sat on old wooden benches in the yard. We were in a Muslim village sharing the gospel. One man from the village was against the people meeting with us, but the ones who attended services told him to leave the church people alone. They'd never heard the message before and wanted to learn more about Jesus.

It was a blessing to help distribute the clothes and other items to the people. The adults' faces lit up as much as the children's did with excitement at seeing all the items neatly organized on long tables for them to pick through. One little girl found the frilly lilac skirt my granddaughter, Zoe had outgrown. The young child grabbed it in a hurry and held it tightly to her chest, bursting in happiness. Max, one of our grandsons, sent shoes he could no longer wear. The little Palawan boy that scooped them up, put them on his feet and pranced around with a big smile, proud to show them off.

The Harvest Is Ready

The only limitation to planting more churches was enough qualified laborers to meet the cries of the people. Opportunities abounded. The team from BPBC was willing to do without to reach more people, but there were only so many people available to send.

The west side of the island was farther away and harder to reach. A member of our church had a relative who lived on the west side, so a team went to her village and shared Christ with her and her people. She asked that we send someone to teach them the Bible weekly. Rick and Joe prayed and sought the Lord for a qualified Bible teacher to send, but our resources were spent. After months of no one going there, she asked, "Do we have to die before you'll send someone to teach us God's Word?"

Rick expressed to me how this kept him awake some nights. The west side of the island had been his burden since he served as a missionary pilot. It's the area where he saw scattered nipa huts isolated throughout the impenetrable forest and wondered how we would ever reach these scattered tribes.

Until the Lord raised up men with a knowledge of the Scriptures who could lead the church plant, it was necessary to wait. A new Christian would not know how to deal with the fierce adversity that would no doubt be waged against him or have enough Bible knowledge to properly teach the Word. First Timothy 3:6 says, "Not a novice, lest being lifted up with pride he fall into the condemnation of the devil." We would wait on the Lord and continue to pray.

With our partner church in the mountain of Tatandayan, the Lord opened a door for our evangelistic team to go to remote tribes where no one had gone with the gospel. The men first made the three-hour hike to Tatandayan. There, the Lord provided a much needed Palawano guide. He spoke the Palawano dialect and knew where the tribes lived hidden in the forest jungles. These tribes were territorial, which could endanger the team's lives without the ability to explain their presence.

For eight days the men climbed up, down, and through the tough, snake and mosquito-infested mountains. The team spent seven to nine hours per day cutting their way through thick brush to different villages. In their backpacks they carried food, medicine, Tang (a powdered orange juice), a cooking pot, paper goods, and pictures of Bible stories. A tent for sleeping at nights hung on one man's shoulder.

Before entering any of the villages, the guide went ahead to call out to the tribe to let them know strangers were approaching. He asked permission from the chieftain to enter. Once given permission, the men entered and treated the sick with medicines and then taught a Bible lesson in the morning and

211

evening. "It was challenging to cover creation all the way to the cross in one lesson," Jeth commented.

The men chopped their way through briars with *bolos* to get to the next village. I watched a video of the team crossing a large ravine by stepping sideways on a tree trunk while hanging onto a vine from a nearby tree to keep from falling into the deep canyon.

At one tribal village, all the people ran and hid in the forest when the men arrived except for the elderly and nursing mothers. The guide persuaded the people to return and guaranteed that they were in no danger. The team shared Christ with that group and the next day hiked another eight hours to a different village nestled in the green forest.

In this place, the team mixed the orange powdered juice with water and handed each Palawano a paper cup with the juice. Fe shared with me that after one sip, the people held the cup in their hands but didn't drink it.

Jeth asked, through his guide, "Why aren't you drinking your juice? Don't you like it?"

They replied, "Yes, we like it very much. It is our first time to drink colored water that tastes so good. If we drink it all at once, it will be gone and we want it to last longer."

Jeth explained, "The colored water you like so much is good, but there is even better water than this. The Creator God can give you Living Waters that will last forever." Then he told them of the lovely Lord Jesus, our Savior.

Fe challenged me with this. "The next time you drink your orange juice, think of the Palawano tribes who still need reached with the gospel and pray for them."

Though the team preached in several villages, only a few trusted Christ. Many said, "We will think about what you've told us because it is our first time to hear this message that sounds peculiar to our ears."

Out of eight tribes, only two people had previously heard the gospel. The two who had heard the message had heard it only once. The men returned to Brooke's Point in much need of a shower, a good meal, and a bed. They were weary but rejoicing they'd had the opportunity to give hope to men, women, and children who'd never heard of the good news of Christ. Now they'd heard of the Creator God, who loved them so much that He provided His only Son, Jesus, to be their Savior. Will they believe? Tatandayan Bible Church could follow up.

When Rick showed the DVD of their evangelistic trip to unreached tribes in churches, it took two years before he could show the video without tears swelling up in his eyes. His hope of seeing the gospel go to the unreached was coming true one tribe at a time.

Aribungos (Ah ree boong us)

A team of local workers from BPBC traveled north of Brooke's Point and held fourteen daily vacation Bible schools at Aribungos. Hopes are that a local church will be raised up in the place as Bible studies are now being held there.

Mt. Kalwe (Kahl wee)

The church was asked to send a team to Mt. Kalwe to an unreached tribe. They hiked for a day up and down mountains to reach the village. After sharing the gospel with tribe, the leader said he and his people had never heard of Jesus. They'd never heard of heaven or hell either. Before the men from BPBC left, the chieftain asked them to come back but to inform them first. There were two hundred others in the mountains he wanted to invite the next time to hear the message. Isaiah speaks of God's plan to bring Israel back to Himself and says in Isaiah 52:7, "How beautiful upon the mountains are the feet of him that bringeth good tidings, —that publish peace, that publish salvation."

It takes the feet of a Christian soldier to publish salvation. This is reinforced by Paul's burden for his people in Romans 10:15. "How then shall they call on him in whom they have not believed? And how shall they believe in him of whom they have not heard? And how shall they hear without a preacher? And how shall they preach, except they be sent? As it is written, How beautiful are the feet of them that preach the gospel of peace and bring glad tidings of good things!" Can I see beauty as God sees it, not with my eyes, but with my heart?

Pangobilia (Pah ngu bee lee ah)

When the son of the vice mayor in Brooke's Point trusted Christ, his life changed. He became burdened for the people who rented homes from him at Pangobilia. More than eighty people attend weekly services to be taught the Scriptures. Many have received Christ as their personal Savior through the preaching, and plans are in the works for it to become a local church.

214

Suring (Sooh ring)

Suring is a new outreach that started from our young people holding a Bible club for the children. The people liked what they heard and wanted to learn more about the Bible. Weekly studies are being held there.

Balabac (Bah lah bahk)

The harvest truly is plenteous, but we need more laborers. Recently nineteen of the church family went to Balabac to share the gospel per the request of a schoolteacher in Brooke's Point. She's from the island and has family there. The Balabac Strait connects the South China Sea with the Sulu Sea and is part of the Palawan province but is separated by the channel.

The small island is one hundred per cent Muslim of the Molbog tribe. After a twelve-hour trip by jeepney, tricycles, and a small boat through crocodile-infested waters, they arrived and rode motorcycles to their destination. They were told if someone is missing on the island, the assumption is the person has been eaten by a crocodile. The people who live there said they had no life and were just waiting to die. Their conditions were hopeless. Not even merchants go there to trade their goods.

Our team took food and shower shoes, what I call flipflops, for the people. They taught them the message God has for all men. Each day they expected the people to come to Bible study in their new shower shoes, but they still came barefoot. Jeth asked them why they weren't wearing the shower shoes. They answered, "We want to save them for a special occasion." The next time the church plans to take two pair of flipflops for each person they meet.

The group did a survey in the area with hopes of one day starting a church there. A few made professions of faith. The people welcomed them to return and looked forward to their next visit. When it came time to leave, the people said, "Thank you for giving us hope."

BPBC carries a strong burden for these people and won't rest until all have been reached with the message of salvation across southern Palawan.

Something to Ponder

Who are you and I giving hope to? Where would we be if people stopped sharing the gospel in our country? God calls the faithful to courage. He asks, "Is my hand shortened at all, that it cannot redeem? Or have I no power to deliver?" (Isaiah 50:2)

Satan loses a portion of his power with each person that trusts Christ and each church that's planted. He's not omnipresent like God and has to divide his forces, weakening his hold where the gospel goes.

God's light quenches Satan's darkness of hopelessness. You and I help extinguish the darkness by spreading God's truth. The Lord is ready and able to be a refuge and strength and people's hope and promise of eternal life. We can't assume everyone knows the message even in America.

May God give us boldness to speak as we ought to speak with a clear message of hope and acceptance in the Beloved. Let's surrender all we are to Him and let Him make our lives count for eternity. My soul sings to Thee, O Lord my God, and my Creator, how great Thou art! "For the Lord is great, and greatly to be praised: he is to be feared above all gods." (Psalm 96:4)

Prayer

Oh, God, who am I that You should bless me with a knowledge of Yourself and eternal life. There are no words to express the magnitude of Your love and mercy towards me in the giving of Your Son. Help me appropriate Your power and open my mouth with boldness and grace even in the furnace of affliction.

May my worship be pleasing in Your sight. May You delight in me because I fear You. Might I praise You for the wonderful works You've done in the hearts of men. Thank You for the joy that fills my heart when I see people without hope find hope in Christ. My soul magnifies You and I rejoice in my salvation. Thank You for Your mercy that is on all who fear You from generation to generation. You are full of grace and truth and have made Yourself available to us for the asking. To God be the glory. In Jesus' name I pray. Amen.

CHAPTER EIGHTEEN

Passing the Baton

When we're young, becoming old seems far away. We have our whole life in front of us and we don't realize how fast our time will go. We busy ourselves with the demands of today until the future is here. If we planned ahead, we're ready to pass the baton to the younger generation that is now grown and let them run with it.

BPBC's children served others as they grew up in the church. They ran errands and cleaned the grounds alongside their fathers and mothers. It became an honor for them to look after the needs of the pastor and the church family. They saw the joy the evangelistic teams had going out to reach the unreached with the gospel and wished they were old enough to join them. Now grown, they'd readied themselves to take hold of the leadership and run the race with patience.

With the multitude of outreach ministries growing, we needed to increase ministries on the home front to meet the demands without stretching ourselves too thin. A friend who visited the work once said, "I've never seen so much done with so little."—Amy Hearing

First on the agenda was the need for a new church building for BPBC.

The same cement block building Fe found hidden behind tall grasses twenty-one years earlier had aged and was no longer safe to meet in. Jeth told me he encouraged his father and the church to think big and build a large, beautiful church for the Lord. The people believed it could serve as a testimony to Christ, and others, of their devotion and gratitude to Him. Considering that most of the people, including Joe and Fe, lived in nipa huts, it would be a huge testament of their dedication for the cause of Christ.

Although opposition grew among a few in the church to build a grand building, the church family as a whole had a mind to work and gave themselves to the task ahead. Since they didn't have money, they'd build the church from what God put in their hands.

Be Amazed

Construction began. The men dug the foundation by hand. When it came time to cover it with gravel, they expected to do the back-breaking work of spreading it with shovels. Resourceful and persuasive Fe found another way.

She hopped on her motorcycle and hurried to the area government trucks were working on road repairs. She explained the church situation to the government workers and asked if they'd be so kind to bring their dump truck by our church and spread the gravel.

I laughed when she told me the men agreed to do it. To the amazement of all, the government vehicle pulled onto the property and spread the gravel.

She laughed with me and added, "I was very popular with the men at church that day."

The task of building required the people have a lot of patience and faith. When they were able to purchase materials, they built. When there were no funds or materials, they waited until the Lord provided.

When Rick and I attended the twenty-fifth church anniversary, we held services for the first time in the unfinished building. After five years, phase 1 was complete, but the building was only a cement shell with a roof. The benches we built when we first moved into the old building sat inside the bare space.

Joe and Fe's son, Jay flew in from Manila for the anniversary celebration. He worked as a news producer for a popular TV station and used his salary to support the church. While at the church he saw it needed a project manager. Two years later, he quit his job and moved back home with his parents to help in the ministries of BPBC, with no income. Phase 2 of the construction began with Jay on site. He became the project manager of not only the new building but all our church projects including the outreaches. He organized teams for the jobs that needed done.

Rick became the field representative for Southern Palawan Ministries and introduced churches to the various ministries of BPBC. With a project manager in place and Rick helping raise funds, much more was able to be accomplished through good management of time and resources.

Joe wanted all the church family to feel a part of the new church building, so he encouraged even the Sunday school children to donate towards it. If they had a centavo or two, less than a penny in value, they gave it until enough was collected to purchase one piece of tile for the flooring. Every member felt good—no great! —that they had a part of the new church being built for the Lord.

Church volunteers raked stones out of the dirt yard to prepare the land to plant grass. The owner of vacant land across the street gave us permission to remove sections of carabao grass to plant in the churchyard. Women dug up a handful of the grass by its roots using a small garden tool until they had enough to fill the churchyard. The grass was known for spreading fast.

I wanted to help the ladies plant grass. We sat under a large tarp to protect us from the sun. We trimmed each handful of grass and its roots with scissors. I was impressed by the tedious work they did planting neat rows of grass with great patience and sweet attitudes.

The mosquitos swarmed around us and bit our bodies nonstop. I made a compassionate comment to one of the faithful ladies, Didong *(Dee dung)*. "The work is difficult."

She smiled kindly and looked my way, "I don't mind. It's for the Lord." Then she saw my beet-red face. I'd only been working thirty minutes. These ladies worked all day for a solid week planting grass in the heat.

Didong was a nurse and knew my body wasn't accustomed to the tropics. She insisted I stop to prevent a sunstroke. I didn't want to stop, but the work was too hard for me. When they finished the task, it wouldn't be long before the grass would take root and the churchyard would be covered with luxurious green grass.

The men mixed the rocks they'd raked from the yard with cement and made borders for the flower gardens. Others found red bricks and hauled them to the church to make an attractive, large sign with the church's name out front. The ladies adorned it with more plants and flowers. Most were brought from a field or their own yard.

It's inspiring to be with them and see what they create. Besides a couple generous donations, the church was built with money from the people. Some didn't have much money, but they gave of themselves in abundance. The completed church building took ten years. It lost the stigma of being the "poor church."

Mrs. Morrison is with the Lord, but when she was on Palawan, she told Fe, "When you build your new church, be sure to give it lots of lights because people are drawn to light." They followed through with plenty of lights in the auditorium and outside the church.

After its completion, the people constructed a prayer garden on one side of the church. Ladies added flowering plants and the men hauled large rocks from the rivers to make a corner waterfall. A few of our old benches were placed outside along the side of the church under the windows and new pews were built for the auditorium. On Wednesday night prayer services, I love going outside to the garden to pray. In the background I hear the sound of the waterfall. It's a charming and calming place, available anytime. The beauty of the people's lives is seen in their work.

A few years later they added a simple outdoor kitchen. With a joyful laugh Fe said, "Thank you for building my kingdom." The ladies have so much fun cooking together for the fellowships.

Camp Ministry

Jay's organization skills made him an excellent camp director. BPBC offers camp each year for every age group. Many of the current adult leaders in our church were saved as young people at camp. They are some of our church's most faithful servant-leaders. Jaimah was one such camper and told us her story.

Her Muslim father learned she attended BPBC and became so irate that he threatened to behead her. With a *bolo* in her father's hand holding it up ready to strike her, she courageously declared, "If you kill me, I will be with my Lord in heaven."

He paused.

In a fit of anger, he flung the *bolo* across the concrete floor. It hit with loud and boisterous bangs. He yelled and swore, "I'm warning you, don't ever take your brothers to that church, or I will keep my word and behead you," then walked away fuming.

Music interested Jaimah, so she asked her father if she could go to Manila and study at Bob Jones Memorial Bible College (BJMBC). She explained, "Since my father loved music and it would take me away from BPBC, he allowed me to study there. I didn't tell him it was a Bible college, or that my true purpose for going was to learn more about God. In my second year, I am very distressed and feel guilty for not telling the truth. I prayed for courage to be honest with him. I'm very afraid and my flesh literally shakes.

"I asked my father for a moment of talk. As I'm telling him the truth, I'm shaking and I almost can't talk. My voice is also shaking, but at last I said, 'Please forgive me, papa, for not telling you the truth that I am in Bible school.'

"He then replied that he already knew that from one of my uncles. He was really hurt at first but realized he can't do anything about me pursuing my Christian life. He forgave me."

Jaimah prayed that the Lord would change his heart. Today she feels free and praises the Lord for His powerful and mighty works in the hearts of unbelievers because her father permits her brothers and her to attend BPBC.

When Jaimah graduated from BJMBC, she returned to BPBC as our trained and gifted pianist. She also helped direct the choir and does a masterful job. Both of her brothers trusted Christ and were baptized at BPBC when Rick and I were there holding our annual Bible conference. Seven in all were baptized that morning. No more walks to the Sulu Sea because our new church had its own baptismal tank.

Camps Abroad from the Wilds in North Carolina gave our camp counselors exceptional training to better equip them in the ministry to campers. Currently, BPBC owns about five acres of undeveloped land in the foothills that they hope to develop and use for the camp. Just as the people waited for funds to build the new church building, they'll wait on the Lord to provide for the camp.

Master's Creation

Deborah quit her job as a professor to go full time in the ministry at BPBC. With no support, she moved into her parent's nipa home along with her brother Jay. She founded Master's Creation as a ministry to help the local church thanks to her experience in mass communications. She trained those interested in how to print materials such as bulletins and Sunday school materials for the church and its outreach ministries but moved from there into a media ministry and audiovisual taping of special events. The young people were getting a degree in mass communications without charge.

They made excellent DVDs of the ministries for Rick to show churches. The interaction of people seen on the DVDs puts you there with the people. No matter how much you try to explain the people, their work, and the area, seeing them is a greater storytelling venue.

Because of Deborah's contacts with former students at Palawan State University, our church was given ninety minutes of radio broadcasting on Sunday mornings. Different men record their messages beforehand and broadcast to five main towns on the island. Feedback tells us God has used it to bless people. Rick got to tell the story on the radio of the plane crash and share how God used it as the springboard to start BPBC.

Affordable cell phones have been made available on the island. Most families have at least one. This is how people listen to our Christian radio station. Our church bought one cell phone for each outreach so they could listen to the broadcasts but also make communication easier between them and BPBC workers.

Several young adults were now trained in Media Ministries, and it's a good thing. The ministry exploded. Master's Creation has a new director, Vanvan. He also works as an assistant pastor at BPBC. The young people involved in the Master's Creation ministry provide professional videos where we can watch the climb of the evangelistic teams to the mountains and meet the people they've gone to reach. We can see services at BPBC and observe those being ordained into the ministry. It's a joy to see the campers play Tug of War with a rope as the waves of the Sulu Sea splash in the background. The audiovisual ministry puts you on the island.

Literacy

At the same time Deborah started to train others in mass communications, she carried a burden for the Palawanos in the mountains to learn to read. If they could read the Bible, their spiritual lives could develop as they gained more knowledge of Christ.

She and a couple volunteers hiked the two-hour trek twice a week to the Tatandayan village to start a literacy class and back again. She wrote the program since they spoke Palawano and wouldn't know English or Tagalog. Both adults and children attended classes. Palawanos from other mountain villages hiked as many as two hours to be able to attend her classes.

When a Christian was elected mayor of the town, her administration built a school at Tatandayan for the Palawano tribes and hired the ladies helping Deborah to be their full-time teachers.

Bible School

Jeth graduated with a master's degree in theology and was recommended to be a recipient of a scholarship program at Bob Jones University in Greenville, South Carolina. Since he believed a doctorate would equip him to establish a Bible school for his people, and a Christian academy for the community, he was grateful for this incredible opportunity.

While studying in Greenville, he visited people he knew from Brooke's Point who lived in New York. When there, he became reacquainted with a former student he grew up with. At one time she had wanted to be a nun. Jeth led her to the Lord and she became a faithful and active Christian in her New York church. They became interested in each other.

Each summer break from Bible college, Jeth returned to Palawan to help his father in the church. While there, the church leaders in the outreaches told him they were eager for the Bible school to start. Although we were thrilled to see the local men grow and take leadership roles, just as Rick and Joe had envisioned, it was church policy not to ordain them as pastors until they were trained in the Scriptures.

Over the next two years of study in Greenville, Jeth wrote a manual to use in BPBC's future Bible school as his thesis. He called it, "Groundbreaking: A Manual for Pioneer Church Planting among the Palawano Tribe." This completed his doctorate.

On his way back to Brooke's Point, he flew to New York and proposed to Jane with her father's permission. Her pastor gave Jeth a good report of her character and faithfulness. Jeth and Jane went home to Brooke's Point and wedding bells rang a few months later.

Dr. Jeth Malacao was ordained as the senior pastor of BPBC upon his return. Pastor Joe became pastor emeritus. He'd had a stroke a few years earlier and needed Jeth to assume the role.

The church waited ten years to establish Southern Palawan Fundamental Bible School (SPFBS) and now Pastor Jeth was prepared to start it. Men from our church who acquired Bible degrees aided in the Bible school as teachers with Pastor Jeth as its director.

Pastor Jeth's eldest brother, Jojo, gave financial support to build a new building to train future pastors and missionaries. Besides a Bible school, it is used as Sunday school classrooms, church fellowships, and conferences.

SPFBS's grand opening thrilled us. Rick and I longed for this day and rejoiced in it. Men in various villages as well as Brooke's Point are able to learn Bible doctrine, biblical principles, church government, and practical Christian living to help prepare them for leadership in their villages and outreaches. The students support the people in the outreaches and help pass out tracts, invite the people to services, and come alongside and help them build their churches. They train others in the Word, discipleship, and counseling so one day they can be an independent church.

Women play a major role in evangelistic ministries and also take classes to learn to counsel using the Scriptures. They teach children and conduct ladies' classes. They are also part of the evangelistic teams that go to new areas for the spread of the gospel until all of Southern Palawan has been reached.

Pastor Jeth's dissertation manual is an effective tool in the Bible school to inform future pastors and missionaries of the Palawano tribes' history, customs, beliefs, and religious traditions. Here is an excerpt from the training manual:

"Rituals practiced by the Palawanos are linked to agriculture and healing. Rice is the main crop and controls the annual cycle of their rituals. Ceremonies are included with the ritual. Before the land is cleared for planting, permission is asked from the spirits to borrow the land since the spirits own it. Another ceremony before planting the rice, and again before harvesting the crop is held. The leader of the family calls for the spirits of the dead in order to beseech their favor for an abundant harvest." *(Groundbreaking: A Manual for Pioneer Church Planting among the Palawano Tribe by Dr. Jethro C. Malacao; p. 36)*

Mission Board

With students in the Bible school, the missionary candidates needed a mission board to go out under. The church began Southern Palawan Missions Board (SPMB) to give backing and accountability to those being sent from our church. The battle for souls is accomplished by faithful servants who know the Lord goes before them to prepare the way.

Something to Ponder

When we consider the trials we face in the Lord's work, they would be more than we could endure apart from God's grace. He keeps us faithful to His calling as he promised in the verse, "Faithful is he who calleth you who also will do it." (1 Thessalonians 5:24)

Because of His faithfulness, we can see the fruit of our labor if we don't quit when trouble comes. How thankful I am for His faithfulness because without it we can't receive the unimaginable blessings God has for us.

What blessings can you name from severe trials in your own life? We see them by the eyes of faith. But once they're over, we can often see what the Lord did in us and for us that blessed others too. "For none of us liveth to himself, and no man dieth to himself." (Romans 14:7)

If our lives are saturated with Scripture, we'll have the mind of Christ and be led to triumph through difficulties. The battle will be won or lost in the mind. A sound mind will sustain us on the path He wants us to walk.

The treasures discovered in the darkness can be known only through difficulties. The fruit of peace and joy through long-suffering grows in hardships. We see that His grace is sufficient and results in His glory.

"But they that wait upon the Lord shall renew their strength; they shall mount up with wings as eagles; they shall run, and not be weary; and they shall walk, and not faint." (Isaiah 40:31) We can't imagine what God will accomplish through our lives when we let Him rule in our hearts.

Prayer

Oh, Lord, my God and Creator of all that is, what can I say to all You are for me? As I turn in dependence upon You, You delight in Your servant. Thank You for Your faithfulness that never fails. You are trustworthy and keep Your promises. I'm grateful for the grace You give to live a Christian life that prospers, flourishes, and is fulfilling. By faith, fear is replaced with joyful expectation. I see the marvelous work You continue to do. How great Thou art and greatly to be praised. When troubles come in like a flood, may I look towards heaven and see You through the eyes of faith and not be moved. All is well because You are on the throne, and my hope is in You. In Jesus' name I pray. Amen.

CHAPTER NINETEEN

Change, Mystery, and Surprise

At the beginning of Rick and Joe's ministry, Joe teased Rick that Brooke's Point wasn't the end of the world, but you could see it from there. Rick likes to joke and repeated the joke to the Bible school students years later. None of them knew what he was talking about for it no longer rang true. Not only had the people changed but so had the town.

It's a fact that truth changes us. It changes the way we think, and thus act. With a change in lives comes a change in families, communities, and even a country. On Palawan, we had freedom to teach the Bible and witness wherever we went. People heard the gospel and some trusted Christ.

Hearing about God and reading about Him for one's self made a difference in the spiritual growth of the people and the stability of the church. The core group had an evident maturity and confidence in Christ that added steadfastness to their faith.

The whole province of Brooke's Point benefited when the Christian niece of Pastor Joe, Maryjean Feliciano was elected mayor. "When the righteous are in authority, the people rejoice." (Proverbs 29:2) She directed her administration to help the people and improve their lives.

The dusty, worn look the town once held is in the past. The dirt roads have been paved and additional streetlights added. A few cars are seen on the streets and paint adorns many of the concrete buildings, giving the place a cleaner and more modern look. An evacuation center and a covered courtyard were raised in the city's square. Even Pastor Joe's favorite banana bread is now sold at the market. Many in Brooke's Point never learned to bake since they didn't own an oven.

Better medical care is available with more doctors and two new hospitals. Education has improved and more young people are able to finish school. Cement houses are being built in place of nipa huts, including the parsonage where Joe and Fe live. For years they battled black bugs eating the nipa walls of their house until a parsonage of concrete and steel could replace it.

Swamps in the area were drained to remove stagnate waters where malaria mosquitos bred. It's nice to go there and not have to sleep under a mosquito net anymore.

The mayor's administration prioritized the welfare of the indigenous people in the mountains and erected more schools. Her administration improved food programs for the needy and put in water systems. Several hanging bridges now cross rivers at the foothills so Palawanos can travel to the lowlands to trade their goods even when the rivers are high. This gives a better flow of the supply and demand need. Fishermen benefit from more trade agreements to export their fish.

Mayor Feliciano ran against a Muslim man for her second term in office. Muslims from other places traveled to Brooke's Point to elect their candidate. Jay made a video of the mayor's accomplishments and posted it on Facebook for the people to watch on their cell phones. When the votes were counted, the people rejoiced to see she had won again, even with big money from a mining company paid to defeat her.

The road from Puerto Princesa to Brooke's Point still had potholes and bridges out, but each year more progress is made to have the entire road paved. The government has begun construction on a three-lane highway and an airport in the province of Brooke's Point since it will become the capital of Southern Palawan once the island is divided into three parts, northern, central, and southern.

More churches, two more banks, plus a better variety of supplies are available in town. McDonald's isn't in Brooke's Point yet, but it's been in Puerto Princesa for several years. It's as popular overseas as it is in America, and its food tastes the same.

The mayor attends BPBC as often as her job allows. On one of our mission trips, Rick approached her after church and made a request. "Is it possible to build a road up the mountain to reach Cabangaan and Tatandayan? With her gracious smile she replied. "I'm working on it."

The dirt path cleared for a road is dreadful and not safe to travel during rains, but it's a beginning. Rick and others had a few wipeouts on their motorcycles getting to the villages.

Businesses have grown and new businesses moved into the town. Mayor Feliciano will be the first to tell you that the improvements have been by God's grace and goodness.

One blessing in the town is the excitement the people get from the annual display of Christmas lights at BPBC. Brightly colored Christmas lights hang and glow in the night's darkness, attracting people from all over. The church writes a play and the choir prepares a cantata to celebrate the birth of Christ. Christmas is a big deal at BPBC, giving another venue to share the gospel.

Deaf Ministry

Perhaps the lights caught the attention of the deaf because a few started to attend the church. Pastor Jeth believed the Lord sent them, and therefore, it became our responsibility to learn sign language. Three young adults volunteered to learn the deaf language. Each service they take turns sitting in the church balcony with the deaf to give them the message in sign language.

BPBC Sends Out Missionaries

Our outreach ministries in the mountains advanced when a couple were called to Cabangaan as missionaries. Excitement filled the church as we ordained our first missionary couple. Roniel Pitago with his wife, Dolly. They met in Bible school and Roniel brought his wife back to Brooke's Point to minister under Southern Palawan Ministries. They went to Cabangaan to help the church become independent. They succeeded at their mission.

With Missionary Roniel at Cabangaan, Pastor Jeth established an extension of SPFBS at Tatandayan and put Roniel in charge of classes. He helps train the Palawano students in God's Word and evangelism. The school building Mayor Feliciano's administration built for the Palawanos doubles as a training center for the Bible school. Putting an extension of our Bible school in the mountains made it possible for more Palawanos to train for the work of evangelism and church planting.

Roniel and Dolly plan to work on the west side of the island when Cabangaan has its own pastor. It was his aunt who asked, "Will we have to die before you send someone to teach us the Word of God?"

Christian Academy

Pastor Jeth organized a Christian academy for the children with assistance from Mrs. Nel (Beth) Guiang and Deborah Malacao. Southern Palawan Christian Academy (SPCA) started with preschool and kindergarten and now has grade four with one hundred and sixty-three students. The plan is to add one grade per year until we have all twelve grades.

Jay's team created a decorative playground for the students out of old tires, vehicle seats, wood, and empty paint cans. The colorful playground sits on land where we once gathered carabao grass for our churchyard.

The government recognized SPCA as the model private school for Palawan. The heads of the Department of Education in the province came to visit the academy. Both the superintendent and director awarded it as the best governing private school on the entire island. Deborah is on SPCA's board and was chosen to be on the Palawan board for private schools. She studied Christian education in the States with plans to become the administrator for SPCA.

Due to the school's growth, the church needed more property and purchased more land beside the church. The future goal is that one day a four-story building will be built there for the academy.

A Mystery Solved

A member of Brooke's Point Bible Church visited her brother who lives in the village where the new blue Kawasaki motorcycle sat after the plane crash. It had been thirty-four years since the incident. He told her he'd heard from the Palawanos at Mt. Saray that there had been a plane crash. The tribe told him Pilot Reeck's plane hit the side of the mountain with a violent smash. He relayed the details of the crash to her.

She said, "That story sounds familiar. Pastor Searls had a plane crash. That's how our church started."

They put two and two together and figured out that Pilot Reeck (Rick) and Pastor Searls were the same person.

Rick and I were on the island, so she rushed to the ridge where we stayed to tell us the news. Her brother informed the people at Mt. Saray that Pilot Reeck was alive and in town. They thought maybe he'd died since he'd never returned to the village. The tribe wanted to see him and he wanted to see them too.

Her brother brought seven of them to our place in town. It's hard to explain the emotions that ran through us. We thanked them for helping Rick that day down the mountain. We met the current chieftain who was ten years old when he saw *Tutubi* crash.

While we ate together, we rehearsed the events surrounding the crash of the dragonfly through a translator. Pastor Jeth said the story they told was identical to all Pastor Searls had described over the years. It was an incredible experience to be with one of the Palawano warriors who had guided Rick down the mountain, still alive and able to recall the ordeal. All seven Palawanos professed to know the Lord.

To show them our gratitude, Pastor Jeth and others from BPBC hiked to the mountain to share clothing we'd shipped earlier from the States. While there, the people showed him the place where the Super Cub crashed. Pastor Jeth shared the story with us, then remarked, "It is a miracle you're alive."

An Unsolved Mystery

Rick and I wanted to go to the home of our friend's brother and look again at the area where Rick had seen the blue motorcycle.

We were taken to the little village where warriors left Rick after they guided him down the mountain. He stood there alone and injured at the time. He pointed me to the area where he'd seen the new Kawasaki motorcycle leaning against a hut. I gazed at the spot.

Inside the brother's hut sat the barrel the missionary's wife had in her hut at Mt. Saray. She'd given Rick a cloth from it for him to press against his bleeding face. Rick asked the brother, "Did you hear of a new blue Kawasaki motorcycle in the village the day of the crash?"

"No."

"Did anyone talk about a blue Kawasaki that needed repaired?"

"No."

Rick explained that the owner of it drove him out of this village after the crash happened.

"I've never heard of a new blue Kawasaki being in this village, or of anybody owning one."

In a small village everyone knows each other. If the man had been a stranger, they would be talking about a strange face in the area. No one except Rick saw the cycle and the man who drove him out of the village. Whoever he was remains a mystery.

Rick and I asked ourselves, *Had God sent an angel that day to rescue him?* We may never know until we get to heaven.

Back to the Beginning

Six more years had passed since our reunion with people from Mt. Saray. A former member of the previous church in the village had destroyed it. He believed evil spirits told him his wife was sick because of his affiliation with the church, so he tore it down. The man hoped with the church gone his wife would get well. Instead, she died. It exposed the truth that it wasn't because of the Christian church she'd been ill. This thinking probably needed to be erased before they'd permit another church in the village.

After this, the chieftain asked Pastor Jeth if we would start a church for them and teach them God's Word. We were overjoyed at the opportunity to work with this tribe as long as we weren't infringing on another man's work. They assured us we weren't. The most recent missionaries who left often attended our church and stated they hoped BPBC would continue the work with the tribe. No one planned to work with them anymore.

We were thrilled for the open door to help the tribe learn from God's Word. *The Crash of the Dragonfly* was the seed that gave birth to BPBC and all that has come from its inception, so starting a work with them excited us.

At the first service BPBC held for Saray Bible Church, the chieftain told the people the story of the plane crash. He'd witnessed it. Then he shared with his people that Pilot Reeck would be coming to greet them. They were pleased.

Funds were donated to build a new church, a water well, and a bathroom at Mt. Saray. As they considered where to construct their new church, the people said nothing had been able to grow at the place where the plane crashed forty years earlier. They tried to plant vegetables and other crops, but not even grass would grow there. Yet, all around the area is a literal jungle. All agreed that spot would be the perfect place to build their new church. The ground was already cleared.

Rick and I laughed with joy. I felt like the Lord looked down at me with a smile and said, "Surprise." He took us back to the very village and people where it all started. I'm amazed that the land where the plane hit and slid to a stop had been set aside for such a time as this.

An Eternal Focus

A plane crash would not be the way I'd choose to start a church. Leaving my comfortable home to go through malaria, satanic oppression, opposition from within and without, ridicule, false accusations, threats of war, religious and political opposition, and our children suffering was more rugged than the rocky, rough, snake-infested trails up the Palawan mountains. Yet, how can I do anything but rejoice because the Lord carried us through the deep waters unharmed?

All that seemed against us and the work redounded to the glory of God. He directed events to work in our favor so the cause of Christ could be advanced. BPBC has established thirteen outreach churches, evangelistic teams, camp ministries, a mission board, Bible school, radio ministry, a media ministry, and a Christian academy with copies of the Bible to strengthen and guide their lives. The goal to reach all of Southern Palawan with the gospel moves forward. The story doesn't end with this book.

Genesis 50:20 says, "But as for you, ye thought evil against me, but God meant it unto good, to bring to pass, as it is this day, to save much people alive." Satan meant the crash of the dragonfly for evil—to stop God's work and his worker. But God meant it unto good to save much people alive. Instead of it ending Rick's life and ministry, it became the seed that gave birth to BPBC, the salvation of many, and all the ministries that resulted.

The key that unlocks God's blessings is prayer. It's a humbling experience to be with the people and witness the sincerity of their worship. Before any new church or ministry is begun, they have spent years praying over it. It's amazing to see what God can do with a people who love Him and give unselfishly so others can know of the Savior and have eternal life with Him. How amazing it is to have the privilege to grow in a relationship with the King of kings and Lord of lords.

I told Fe I feel like the work has grown beyond us. She feels the same. It's more than we ever thought to pray for. The right people are in the place of leadership to take the work forward. Pastor Jeth has a team of men who are ordained and work well with him. He has been given an opportunity several times to share a message from the Bible at government events and new business openings.

I cannot say enough good about Pastor Joe and Fe. When Joe experienced serious health problems later in life, I asked how he wanted me to pray for him. Without missing a beat, he answered, "Pray that God would extend my life so I can reach more people with the gospel." Joe and Fe have led many of their people to a saving faith in the Lord Jesus. They've given their all for Christ and His people and taught their children to do likewise.

It's amazing to watch God bring our lives and His work full circle. Our pastor told us that after buffetings come blessings. God has been faithful and brought us to a place of unimaginable blessings.

With the changes in Brooke's Point some things never changed—the love of God's people for the Lord and His Word, the love they exhibit towards each other, and the church on the march to claim more territory for Christ—preaching the gospel to whosoever will.

"For our light affliction, which is but for a moment, worketh for us a far more exceeding and eternal weight of glory; while we look not at the things which are seen, but at the things which are not seen: for the things which are seen are temporal; but the things which are not seen are eternal." (2 Corinthians 4:17-18) These truths, mixed with praying faith, have been anchors for my soul.

The Lord is building His church, "and the gates of hell shall not prevail against it!" (Matthew 16:18) May we do our part for the glory of God until Jesus comes.

Something to Ponder

God is no respecter of persons. Each of us has the privilege to receive God's blessings by reading the truth in Scripture with faith, and obeying its teachings. If we will accept the Bible as God's Words, and not man's, it will change us. Instead of creating our own beliefs, and building a way of life that seems right to us, we can follow the guidebook God gave and live the abundant life promised to His children. It's a life full of purpose that is better than popularity, money, and power. It's a life that counts for eternity.

A man determined to go his own way and ignore God's way can be swayed to follow a false light and be led astray. If we live to please ourselves, we reap the harvest of a wasted life. The Lord loves us and wants us to look, listen, and learn from Him, for what does it matter if we gain the whole world but lose our own soul?

Prayer

Lord, I thank You for the marvelous works You've done and continue to do in the hearts of men, women, and children. I'm amazed by changes You bring to a life, a family, and a community from preaching the gospel. God's Word changes us, but it never changes. Your Word is pertinent for every generation. Joshua 1:8 tells us, "This book of the law shall not depart out of thy mouth; but thou shalt meditate therein day and night, that thou mayest observe to do according to all that is written therein: for then thou shalt make thy way prosperous, and then thou shalt have good success." Where truth goes, His blessings follow. May more and more people look up and see the goodness of God. For Jesus' sake I pray. Amen.

CHAPTER TWENTY

Heart Reflections

This book was written in my voice as a missionary wife. I'd like you to hear the voice of the two men who led in the establishment of Brooke's Point Bible Church, Pastor Joe and Pastor Searls. The following are their hearts' reflections.

Pastor Joe's Reflections

Fe and I felt an emptiness in our Christian lives. I was struck when I read the Apostle Paul's words in Acts 20, particularly verse 27. "For I have not shunned to declare unto you all the counsel of God." God burdened my heart that my people and I needed to be taught the whole counsel of God.

Professing Christians in my area of Palawan knew God loved them, but some didn't understand the seriousness of sin, or even what it was. Others believed those without a knowledge of Christ could be saved if they looked into the heavens and believed there was a God. But even the demons believe God exists, and they won't enjoy heaven. Jesus said no man comes to the Father except by Him.

I desired the kind of church that taught the whole counsel of God and began to pray for one. That's when we met the Searlses. We got to know them as a result of the plane crash. Both of our families believe the Lord put us together.

Pastor Searls taught me the need for the church to hold to the fundamentals of the faith and what they were. He showed me from Scripture our lives and our church needed to be separated from sin and set apart for God. I asked him to pray about planting a church in Brooke's Point and told him I would surely be his partner.

Starting a new church in town was very hard to do and took courage from the Lord. The town was mostly owned by one family and they dominated, even controlled, the leaders of the church my family once attended. It was difficult to separate, knowing it would be considered shameful, but our spiritual hunger made us seek help from Pastor Searls.

The Lord gave me the verse in Deuteronomy 31:6 to encourage me in this mission. "Be strong and of a good courage, fear not, nor be afraid of them: for the Lord thy God, he it is that doth go with thee; he will not fail thee, nor forsake thee."

After a year of prayer, the Lord led the Searlses to plant a church with us. Another year later we started the church together. Nobody who learned of our plan to start a new church in Brooke's Point believed we would make it. Others tried to start another church in town and had been driven away.

Acts 20:24 says, "But none of these things move me, neither I count my life dear unto myself, so that I might finish my course with joy, and the ministry, which I have received of the Lord Jesus, to testify the gospel of the grace of God."

As you read in this book, we experienced trials that only the Lord could help us endure. And you read how God used these trials to give us victory in the work and reach more souls for Him. As Mrs. Searls said, "It would have been impossible to start a church in Brooke's Point if it was not of the Lord." There were many things against us.

Later in the church history I experienced being betrayed by those whom I loved much in the ministry. It was very painful; but if Christ had Judas and Paul had Demas, we also had those in the church who we felt betrayal from. The servant is not greater than His Lord. Because Jesus is with me, I am who I am because of Him who saved me. My life is for Him. "I am crucified with Christ: nevertheless I live; yet not I, but Christ liveth in me: and the life which I now live in the flesh I live by the faith of the Son of God, who loved me, and gave himself for me." I will serve Him until my last breath or until He comes. My house will serve the Lord to the glory of God!

Everything is the Lord's doing and it is marvelous in our eyes as Psalm 118:23 states. I feel privileged to be chosen to serve Him. The joy and peace in serving the King of kings and Lord of lords far surpassed the trials. I have no regrets, only gratitude for His works in my heart and the people of southern Palawan. Hallelujah!

Pastor Searls's Reflections

As I look back on God's call upon our lives and the journey we have taken with Him, I have to say the same as Pastor Joe did, "This is the Lord's doing; it is marvelous in our eyes. This is the day which the Lord hath made; we will rejoice and be glad in it." (Psalms 118:23-24)

I remember how dark the town of Brooke's Point was physically and spiritually when we first moved there. Physically, the darkness came from being in a remote, undeveloped part of the world. The town had two streetlights, if the generator worked. The lack of electricity gave the town a dark and depressed look.

Spiritual darkness permeated the area, especially in the foothills and mountains. A former missionary had planted seed for us to build upon. Many still needed reached with the gospel. "Moreover, brethren, I declare unto you the gospel which I preached unto you, which also ye received, and wherein ye stand; for I delivered unto you first of all that which I also received, how that Christ died for our sins according to the Scriptures; and that he was buried, and that he rose again the third day according to the scriptures." (1 Corinthians 15:1, 3-4)

Speaking to the Galatians in chapter 1:15-16 the Apostle Paul said, "But when it pleased God, who separated me from my mother's womb, and called me by his grace, to reveal his Son in me, that I might preach him among the heathen; immediately I conferred not with flesh and blood."

Paul recognized God's hand on his life from birth. Paul's purpose was to reveal God to others. When God by His Spirit set Paul apart to preach the gospel of Christ, he didn't seek the opinions of others. He knew what the Lord wanted him to do. These verses in Galatians became my life verses, and the purpose of spreading the gospel of the Lord Jesus Christ became my mission.

When I lived on the island, God used these verses in times of turmoil to remind me that the Spirit of God is the One Who separated me and sent me to Brooke's Point, Palawan. He kept me in His will whenever my heart questioned how I got to this place. The Lord sent me there with the same purpose as Paul's—to reveal His Son to people who sat in spiritual darkness.

Second Corinthians 4:3 says, "If our gospel be hid, it is hid to them that are lost." The word hid means to cover up. Spiritual darkness comes as a result of the gospel being hidden.

Second Corinthians 4:4 shows who is responsible for it being hidden. "In whom the god of this world hath blinded the minds of them which believe not, lest the light of the glorious gospel of Christ, who is the image of God, should shine unto them."

Satan and his army of demons blind the eyes of those in bondage to evil to prevent them from seeing Christ Jesus and trusting Him as their Savior. Satan loses control of a life that turns to Christ.

In Galatians 1:16 the word reveal means to take the cover off. My mission was to take the cover off spiritually blinded eyes that the glorious gospel would be seen through preaching. The gospel is the power of God to salvation to all who believe in Jesus, who He is, and what He's done. (Romans 10:9-13)

"For God, who commanded the light to shine out of darkness, hath shined in our hearts, to give the light of the knowledge of the glory of God in the face of Jesus Christ." (2 Corinthians 4:6)

Through preaching the light of the gospel of Christ, spiritual darkness is quenched. I've seen the change God made in people's lives. Villages changed as some trusted Christ and followed His teachings. They are excited about heaven because they have an assured hope of being there. They fill with an assured hope. A smile stretches across their faces that once carried the burdens of the world.

The gospel has been propagated throughout much of Brooke's Point and it is no longer the backwards, dark place it once was. Many now know what it means to live a plentiful life, enjoying possessions money can't buy.

BPBC was built upon Christ and His righteousness, not on any man. All that has been accomplished is by the grace of God and for His glory. The Lord kept the Malacaos and us unified in the mission and faithful to His call.

One of my favorite songs is Great Is Thy Faithfulness. Pastor John Monroe summed it up well for me in a message he preached. "God is faithful to His call, faithful through His testings, and faithful in His protection." Praise His Name! That sums up the testimony of this book. "And let us not be weary in well doing; for in due season we shall reap, if we faint not." (Galatians 6:9)

God's sovereign hand is at work even at times when we are determined to go our own way or lean on our own understanding. The plane crash transformed me and my ministry. God was glorified in the very thing that I looked at with disappointment and dread.

When life starts to take different turns, I learned to accept the change the Lord brings and make the life-changing turn with God by His grace. He can be trusted.

"What shall we say then to these things," such as the crash of the dragonfly? "If God be for us, who can be against us?" (Romans 8:31)

'Tis so sweet to trust in Jesus,
Just to take Him at His Word;
Just to rest upon His promise,
Just to know,
"Thus saith the Lord."

PHOTOGRAPHS

A Church Is Born

Grass airstrip on flight base with housing in background on right

The Searls home on base.

The Searls family during aviation training.

Arriving from town with supplies in the blue Tamara.

Scott and Brad flying with dad to tribal village to deliver supplies.

Safe landing on mountain airstrip.

Rick pointing to dip in mountain range where plane
went down.

The Malacao family—Joe, Fe, Jojo, Jeriel (Jay), Jason, and Jeth.

Building Fe found hidden behind tall grasses. Used as church for 25 years. Inset: Church painted.

Sunday School classrooms the men built with church family gathered for food and games.

Carolyn, Pastor Martin Masitto, Pastor Dale McCallister, and Pastor Searls using tricycle for transportation.

The Searls family in Manila with the boys in Barongs.

The Malacao family with their four sons and daughter, Deborah.

Rick presenting a copy of the Ang Salita Ng Diyos –
The Word of God- to Joe.

Carolyn's transportation to Mt. Cabangaan in a cart
pulled by a Carabao.

Flattened bamboo being woven for the walls of one of the outreach churches. Inset: Tabud Bible Missions.

Calyon and Rick at Matiyaga. Inset: Matiyaga Bible Church today.

Goreto, the witch doctor who became a Christian.

The Malacao family grown and with their first grandson.

Rick Searls and Jay Malacao.

Mayor of Brooke's Point province and Deborah Malacao.

Dr. Jethro Malacao, senior pastor of BPBC with his wife Jane and son, Jabez

Town of Brooke's Point today with inset of Brooke's Point in 1979.

Joe and Fe ready to enjoy one of her home cooked meals with guests.

Brooke's Point Bible Church today with new classrooms along the right front of building. Inset: The Malacaos and Searls.

Southern Palawan Christian Academy with students K4 to grade four with teachers.

Rick, Carolyn, Fe, and Joe holding theme verse of BPBC, I John 4:4.

Map of Southern Palawan, highlighting many of the
places evangelistic teams have gone

Believers at Cabangaan Bible Church holding paper with song *How Can I Fear* by Ron Hamilton translated into Palawano and a copy of the Ang Salita Ng Diyos..

God used The Crash of the Dragonfly to turn tragedy into triumph and give birth to unimaginable blessings, miracles, and salvation to the glory of God. Inset: Front view of crashed plane.

PHILIPPINE RECIPES

from Fe's Kitchen

Chicken Tinola Soup

- 1 whole chicken cut in serving pieces
- 2 tbsp cooking oil
- 1 head garlic, crushed and peeled
- 1 onion cut for sautéing
- Thumb-sized piece of ginger, peeled and cut into strips
- 3 tbsp cooking oil
- 1 whole green papaya, peeled, seeds scraped out, and cubed
- Salt and pepper to taste
- 1 cup pepper leaves (chili pepper leaves found in Asian stores)
- 2 pieces of lemon grass, head crushed and tied together with its leaves
- 5 cups water
- 1 chicken bouillon cube or more for taste

Directions

Heat the oil in pan, sauté garlic, onion, and ginger. Cover and simmer with chicken pieces until water in the chicken is released. Add salt and a dash of ground pepper. When skillet is dry, add water, lemon grass, and chicken cube(s) and bring to a boil. When chicken is tender, add the green papaya and cook until tender. Add salt and pepper to taste. Next add the pepper leaves. Serve hot with freshly cooked steamed rice.

Pork Adobo

- 2 pounds lean pork, cut into cubes
- 1 head crushed garlic
- 2 onions, chopped
- ¼ cup soy sauce
- ¼ cup vinegar
- 2 tbsp brown sugar
- 1 tbsp pepper corn, crushed
- 2 cups water
- 4 bay leaves, crushed in your hand
- 3 tbsp cooking oil

Directions

Marinate pork in soy sauce, vinegar, sugar, half of the garlic, half of the onions, pepper corn and bay leaves for 20 minutes.

Heat oil in pan. Sauté garlic and onion. Add marinated pork, cover, and simmer. Set aside mixed marinate sauce. When pork is dry, add the marinated sauce to allow the pork to absorb it. Then add two cups water until the meat is tender. Serve hot with freshly cooked steamed rice.

Filipino Pepper Steak

- 1 pound beef tenderloin cut in thin serving piece strips
- 2 large white onions cut in half and then quarters
- 3 stalks celery cut diagonally
- 2 green bell peppers cut in half with seeds removed then quartered
- 2 red bell peppers (same procedure as green bell peppers)
- 3 tbsp soy sauce
- 3 tbsp brown sugar
- 3 tbsp cooking oil
- 2 tbsp cornstarch in ½ cup water stirred
- Salt and pepper to taste

Directions

Brown meat in oil. Cover pan and let meat juices come out. When pan is dry, set meat aside.

Add 3 tbsp cooking oil and sauté onion and celery. Add the meat, soy sauce, brown sugar, and water and cover the pan. Simmer ingredients on low until the meat is tender. Then add the green and red peppers. Mix well. Add the mixed cornstarch in water. Mix well. Serve hot with freshly steamed rice.

Fe said, "Enjoy your meal!"

Fried Mackerel

- 5 fish filets
- Cooking oil
- Marinate in juices of one lemon and one lime with salt and dash of ground pepper for 10 minutes

Directions

Heat oil in frying pan. Add marinated fish. Cook until both sides are golden brown. Serve with tartar sauce and freshly steamed rice.

Chop Suey

- 1 small head garlic crushed and peeled
- 1 onion chopped
- ½ cup lean pork cut in thin slices
- ½ cup chicken breast cut thin
- ½ shelled shrimp
- 1 chicken bouillon cube or more to taste
- 3 tbsp soy sauce
- 2 tbsp brown sugar
- 1 cup water
- Salt and dash of ground pepper to taste
- 1 chayote (a small green gourd) peeled and cut in thin pieces
- 2 large carrots peeled and cut in thin pieces
- 2 red bell peppers with seeds removed and cut in strips
- 2 green bell peppers (same procedure as red bell peppers)

- ½ small head of cabbage
- 15 pieces green beans, sliced in half
- 2 stalks celery chopped
- 1 cup small mushrooms cut in half
- 1 can corn drained
- 2 leeks cut similar to green beans separating white from green leaf
- 4 tbsp oil
- 3 tbsp cornstarch stirred into ½ cup water for thickening

Directions

Heat oil in pan or wok. Sauté garlic until golden brown; add onion and cook until tender. Add celery. When it has cooked a while, add pork and chicken. Sauté and then cover pan and simmer. Cook until all pink is gone from meat; then add shrimp. Sauté until shrimp turns pink. Add soy sauce, brown sugar, and dash of ground pepper. Mix well. Add water and chicken cube(s). Cover pan and simmer until meat is tender. Add chayote, carrots, green beans, green and red peppers, white part of leeks. Cover pan and simmer until vegetables are tender but not overcooked. Add mushrooms, corn, cabbage, leek leaves; mix well with vegetables. Add thickening (cornstarch in water). Stir. Taste. Add salt if needed. Turn off stove. Don't cover pan to prevent overcooking. Serve with steamed rice and enjoy!

Sautéed Green Beans and Squash with Shrimp

- 1pound green beans
- 1 small butternut squash, peeled with seeds removed, cut into small bite size pieces
- 1 green bell pepper sliced in strips
- 1 red pepper sliced in strips
- 1 cup shelled shrimp
- 1 small head garlic peeled and crushed
- 1 chopped onion
- 3 tbsp liquid seasoning
- 3 tbsp cooking oil
- Dash of ground pepper
- ½ cup water

Directions

Heat oil in skillet. Sauté garlic, onion, and shrimp; then add green beans, squash, seasoning, green and red peppers with a dash of ground pepper. Cover and simmer. Add water and bring to boil until vegetables are tender.

Serve with steamed rice.

Bico—Sweetened Sticky Rice

- 3 cups sticky rice
- 3 cups water
- 3 cups coconut milk
- 3 cups brown sugar

Directions

Cook sticky rice in water. Set aside. In pan melt brown sugar in coconut milk on low heat until texture is almost sticky. Mix it with the cooked sticky rice and continue mixing on low heat until texture of rice appears oily. Transfer rice to square pan and flatten with spatula. Cool and cut in squares. Serve for snacks.

Buko Salad—Fruit Salad

- 3 cups young coconut shredded
- 1 can fruit cocktail
- 1 can sweetened condensed milk
- 1 can Nestle Cream, or carton of cream or whipped cream.

Directions

In mixing bowl add shredded coconut. Cut tops off the young coconuts and discard the milk. Rub inside each coconut with fresh lemon juice to avoid discoloration. Scrape out the young coconut for salad and place in bowl. Add drained fruit cocktail, milk, and cream. Chill in refrigerator and serve as dessert.

Banana Cue

- 20 cooking bananas
- 2 cups brown sugar
- 3 cups cooking oil
- Bamboo sticks

Directions

Diagonally cut bananas in thirds. Heat 3 cups oil in fryer. Place sliced bananas in oil to deep fry. Once bananas become yellowish, add brown sugar to oil and continue mixing until sugar is melted and the bananas are coated. Drain to remove excess oil. Continue process until all are cooked. Place three or four banana pieces on a stick. Serve hot with coffee.

Banana Turon (Lumpia)

- 10 cooking bananas
- 2 cups brown sugar
- 20 lumpia wrappers
- 2 cups cooking oil
- A little flour and water to make a paste to glue wrappers together after banana is rolled inside each wrapper

Directions

Slice bananas lengthwise in half. Roll each half in brown sugar and put each one in lumpia wrapper. Seal with paste. Heat 2 cups cooking oil. Deep fry the banana lumpia until golden brown. Drain in strainer to remove excess oil. Dust with powdered sugar. Serve hot with coffee or water.

GLOSSARY

Of Tagalog Words

Note: All A's are pronounced with the ah sound.

Ate *(ah teh)*: a word of respect to address an older female relative or friend

Bangka: boat (fishermen used pump boats)

Blowout: celebration with lots of food

Brownout: no electricity

Buko juice *(boo ko)*: the milky water from a young coconut

Carabao *(Cah rah boo)*: water buffalo

Gasul: propane gas

Merienda: snack

Nanay: mommy

Pakikisama *(pah kee kee sah mah)*: getting along well with others. *With a group effort, workload becomes easier through cooperation.*

Palawan the island *(Pah laou wahn)*

Palawan the people *(Pah lah wahn)*

Palawano *(Pah lah wahn o)*: the native Palawan

Palaweno: The people who moved to Palawan from another island

Palenque *(pah link key)*: the outdoor market

Pandesol: a small round bread bun

Pasma: a folk illness unique to the Filipino culture from exposure of cold

Pesos: Philippine money

Kinkis *(kink keys)*: handmade light with a kerosene filled baby food jar and a wick

Sitao *(see towel)*: a long green string bean

Suki *(sue kee)*: personal vendor at the market

Swali *(swah lee)*: split bamboo woven in flat, large sheets and hung as walls on huts

Tamara *(Tah mah row)*: a jeep with a cab that has a bench running along each side

Tarek dance *(tahr ick)*:   the tribes' thanksgiving celebration dance to the spirits

Taupo: a greeting when approaching a home to let the people inside know you are there

Tutubi *(too too bee)*: dragonfly

Trees

Balete *(bah lay tay)*: Many believe this is a sacred

tree that the spirits inhabit and lay offerings of food at it in worship.

Kamagong: Black wood

Ipil— *(E pel)*: extra hard wood

Abbreviations

ASNG: Ang Salita Ng Diyos (The Word of God)

BI: Bibles International

BJMBC: Bob Jones Memorial Bible College

BPBC: Brooke's Point Bible Church

MBC: Maranatha Bible Church

MNLF: Moro National Liberation Front

NPA: New People's Army

PSU: Palawan State University

The Outreach Churches & Mission Works

Aribungos *(Ah ree boon gus)*

Barong Barong *(Bah wrung Bah wrung)*

Cabangaan *(Cah bah ngah ahn)*

Matiyaga *(Mah tee yah gah)*

Puerto Princesa *(Porto Princesa)*

Samarinana *(Sah mahr ee ynah nah)*

Saray *(Sah rye)*: name of mountain range

Sarong *(Sah wrung)* and the witch doctor Goreto *(Gu rae toe)*

Tabud *(Tah bood)*

Tubtub *(Tube tube)*

Tagpinasao-Bilang Bilang *(Tahg pee nah sah oo-Bee lahng Bee lahng)*

Tatandayan *(Tah Tahn dah yahn)*

Filipino: Male

Filipina: Female

The Malacao family: Joe Malacao *(Mah lah cahw)* with wife, Fe *(Feh)*, and children Jojo, Jeriel *(Jay)*, Jason, Jethro *(Jeth)*, and Deborah

ABOUT THE AUTHOR

Carolyn Searls has served alongside her husband, Rick, since 1976, first in missionary aviation when her husband was a jungle pilot, then church planting, and as a pastor. Together they hold annual Bible conferences for the church they helped start in the Philippines. Carolyn is a public speaker and author. Her nonfiction writing won first place in the 2020 Carolina Christian Writers Conference. They are blessed with two sons, a daughter, and eight grandchildren--the joy of their lives.

Made in the USA
Middletown, DE
08 August 2020

14783982R10172